teaching with fire

Teaching with Fire

POETRY THAT SUSTAINS THE COURAGE TO TEACH

Sam M. Intrator and Megan Scribner, Editors

INTRODUCTION BY PARKER J. PALMER AND TOM VANDER ARK

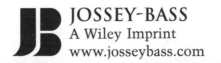

JOSSEY-BASS
A Wiley Imprint
www.josseybass.com

Published by Jossey-Bass
A Wiley Imprint
989 Market Street, San Francisco, CA 94103-1741   www.josseybass.com

Poetry credits are on page 226.

Jossey-Bass books and products are available through most bookstores. To contact Jossey-Bass directly call our Customer Care Department within the U.S. at 800-956-7739, outside the U.S. at 317-572-3986, or fax 317-572-4002.

Jossey-Bass also publishes its books in a variety of electronic formats. Some content that appears in print may not be available in electronic books.

Library of Congress Cataloging-in-Publication Data

Teaching with fire : poetry that sustains the courage to teach / Sam M. Intrator and Megan Scribner, editors.— 1st ed.
    p. cm.
  ISBN 0-7879-6970-2 (alk. paper)
1. Poetry—Collections. 2. Poetry—Translations into English. I. Intrator, Sam M. II. Scribner, Megan.
  PN6101.T36 2003
  808.81—dc22

                                        2003017287

Printed in the United States of America
FIRST EDITION
HB Printing 10 9 8 7

Contents

Holding On 69

Gratitudes

*E*diting this book has been a rare and special privilege. We have been witness to haunting and beautiful conversations between the men and women who teach our children and some of the greatest poets known to the world. As editors we have been on the receiving end of hundreds of e-mail messages and letters in which teachers have written how poems have touched their hearts, enlivened their minds, and sustained their courage.

These commentaries introduce the poems, but they also reveal some inspired truths about teachers. These are dedicated and resolute men and women who believe in the special powers of their work and understand the complex and fragile enterprise of teaching. One cannot listen in on these conversations without feeling that our own children would be fortunate and blessed to have such teachers in their life and learning. For their courage to be honest and their willingness to offer their stories as companions and guides to their colleagues near and far—we are grateful.

The genesis of this book can be traced to the capacity of poetry to energize vision and stir us to imagine what could be possible. An initial meeting of Parker J. Palmer and Tom Vander Ark that began with an exchange of poems quickly led to the convening of a remarkable team of collaborators, all of whom contributed to the conceptualization and completion of the book. Lesley Iura, our wonderful editor from Jossey-Bass, engaged with both the big ideas of the book and the small but imperative details. Rick Jackson, the remarkable man we call our *point guard* because of his ability to lead a team in ways that invited each of us to maximize our own gifts and capacities, always puts us in a position to do our best. We also would like to thank Marcy Jackson and Sharon Palmer for their indispensable contributions in the early and critical stages when we formulated the vision of what this book would become. In the end, this book, more than anything we have ever worked on, embodies what Walt Whitman would recognize as a "varied carol."

Aside from having a team devoted to the idea of this book, we were also very fortunate to have funders and institutions to support us in this work. Our thanks go to the Bill and Melinda Gates Foundation, which generously funded the writing and editing of this book; to the Center for Courage & Renewal for its unflagging support; and to the Fetzer Institute for its support of the Center, the Courage to Teach Program, and this effort. We always felt a special sense of commitment to this book knowing that the royalties will be used to fund scholarship opportunities for teachers to grow and learn.

Our thanks to the Jossey-Bass team, especially to Pamela Berkman, Elisa Rassen, and Hilary Powers, for helping to make this book a reality; and to Sheri Gilbert for tracking down each and every poem and painstakingly making all the corrections and gathering permissions for each one.

Sam writes: Thanks to those teachers in my life who during my youth evoked in me a passion for how words can come together to make beautiful and enduring things: Carmine Giordano, Carl Kornell, Larry Ronaldson, and Ms. Trachman. To my parents, Anna and Neil, to whom I owe my love of story. To my own children: Casey, who is poetry in motion as he careens and bounces through the world; Jake, whose omnivorous love of the written word brings remarkable joy to his father; and Kaleigh, who sees into the world with a poet's capacity to hear the mystery and know the imperceptible. Finally, to Jo: your presence and companionship in my life is the greatest joy I know.

Megan writes: Thanks to my parents, Ginny and Scrib, my first and best teachers. Thanks to my two girls: Anya, who lights up the world with her smile; and Maya, whose unquenchable spirit takes us to the stars. They daily teach me, if I'm smart enough to listen, how to engage the world with wonder, curiosity, and delight. And my very special thanks to Bruce, my husband and best friend, whose good sense, love, and support make it all possible.

Gratitudes

A Note to Our Readers

*T*he poems lie folded and faded in the hidden corners of a teacher's wallet. They are taped to the computer or pinned on a corkboard next to the teacher's desk. Or clipped inside a grading book or written on the cover of a planning binder. Sometimes they are written out in flowing calligraphy and get central billing in the front of a classroom or on the door as a special sign of welcome. Other times they remain bound in well-thumbed books at the bed stand or exist as talismans etched into memory.

We asked teachers to send us these cherished poems. We asked them to write of their special relationship to the poems, to describe how they turn to them for companionship, solace, and wisdom. Through electronic mail, networks, and word of mouth, we spread the word that we were seeking poems that mattered to teachers. We received hundreds of submissions from across the country. Teachers from every level—from those who teach our youngest students to those who teach professionals in graduate school —shared their poems and stories. The response was gratifying and poignant.

In our selection process, we paid attention to both the poem and the teacher's narrative. The poems, written by many of our most celebrated poets—Walt Whitman, Marge Piercy, Wallace Stevens, Langston Hughes, and others—could obviously stand alone. But we believe that the essence of this book involves teachers sharing how they make use of poems to plumb the deeper waters of their work. These teachers have shared how poems can mark a special moment in their life's journey, can help them remember and reconnect with what brought them to their work, and can chide them to dare and dream dangerously about the power of their vocation. As we sat with the collection, a story emerged—teachers across the country, across all levels of the profession, use poetry to keep teaching with fire. This book acknowledges this great truth of teaching—to do it well, to do it justice, requires fire.

Anybody who has ever been a student knows what we mean when we say we need teachers who have fire. *Fire* as in exuberance, vitality, and passion. *Fire* as in being alive for the subjects they teach, being open to and energized by the relationships they forge with their students and their colleagues.

Anybody who has ever taught knows what we mean when we say that teaching can consume us and smother the glow until it dims and flickers low. Most of us came to teaching with a zest for children, an ethic of service, and a mission to forge a better world through the act of teaching others. But to do it well over the span of a school year and the stretch of a career—often within an institution and system punishing to our hearts and passions—is no small task. The forces complicit in dampening that spirit are powerful. Teachers face excessive demands on their time, heightened and manic pressure to raise test scores, and a sense of loneliness that comes from working in a profession that provides little time or opportunity to work with other adults.

Yet if schools are to be places that promote academic, social, and personal development for students, everything hinges on the presence of intelligent, passionate, caring teachers. Teachers have a colossal influence on what happens in our schools, because day after day they are the ultimate decision makers and tone setters. They shape the world of the classroom. Thus we all need educators who each and every day can teach with fire. This book celebrates teachers who know this and have discovered that poetry can help keep their heart in the work and the fire in their soul.

In the poems and stories in the first two sections, "Hearing the Call" and "Cherishing the Work," teachers reflect on the original source of their calling, appreciating and connecting with what they cherish, and through it all renewing their faith in the power of their vocation.

The poems and stories of the next two sections, "On the Edge" and "Holding On," address the struggle against those punishing pressures that often diminish and grind down a teacher's heart.

The fifth and sixth sections, "In the Moment" and "Making Contact," show teachers reclaiming hope and mustering the resolve to say yes to those experiences that rekindle their faith in the vocation of teaching. These teachers are then able to reach out to students, parents, fellow teachers, and administrators, to connect and forge common cause, and by doing so make a difference in the world.

The last sections of poetry, "The Fire of Teaching" and "Daring to Lead," describe how the great gift of teaching is giving heart to yourself and to others to sustain the efforts you believe in. The teachers and educational leaders in this section work to make substantial, heartful change in the world. These poems and stories describe efforts to make our educational institutions effective, inspiring, and impassioned places.

The book concludes with an essay, "Tending the Fire: The Utility of Poetry in a Teacher's Life," that highlights the many practical ways teachers use poetry in their life and work.

This book's intention is to honor the depth and spirit of teaching by providing teachers with a forum in which to share those poems that invite focused attention on their sense of calling, their work, their quiet outrage, or their appreciation for wonder in a child's eye. It has been an honor to help give voice to the stories of so many fine teachers.

Sam M. Intrator
Megan Scribner
July 2003

Introduction

Parker J. Palmer
Author and founder of the "Courage to Teach" Program and the Center for Courage & Renewal

Tom Vander Ark
Executive Director, Education, Bill and Melinda Gates Foundation

One of us was trained as an engineer, the other as a sociologist, two fields infamous for being something less than "poetic." As young men, neither of us was inclined to appreciate poetry. In fact, one of us (who wishes to remain anonymous) once said to his college English professor in a fit of sophomoric frustration, "If this poet has something to say, why doesn't he just come right out and say it?"

But as we have grown steadily older and sporadically wiser, both of us have discovered that poetry offers comfort, encouragement, and more: it is a source of insight and power in our shared concern over the state of public education. That concern led to our first meeting, and when, within an hour, we had both pulled poems out of our pockets to explain what was driving us, we knew we wanted to help bring this book into being.

In the course of doing so, we have learned to our delight that many dedicated teachers and administrators out there on the front lines find solace and strength in poetry. Here you will find some of the poems that sustain them, each with a brief story about how a particular educator has been touched by that poem. We hope that these poems and stories will help the good people in our schools, on whom we all depend, strengthen their commitment to the kind of education that can serve the young—and the whole of society—wisely and well.

That commitment is not easy to maintain in our time. Educational reform has become a vehicle for scoring political points instead of a quest to create learning spaces that are rigorous, relational, and life-giving. In many settings, "learning" has been reduced to test scores, even when the tests are of dubious value. Too many students are warehoused rather than well-served by public schools so massive that the neediest young get lost. Good teachers get lost, too, done in by despair: half of the people who enter this vital profession bail out within the first five years.

Those of us who care about the young and their education must find ways to remember what teaching and learning are really about. We must find ways to keep our hearts alive as we serve students of every class, race, and ethnicity amid discouraging, sometimes devastating, conditions. We must find ways to join with others in public words and actions to help fulfill the promise that education in America has always held.

The Power of Poetry

Poetry has the power to help us do all of this. That claim may sound strange in a culture obsessed with finance, federal policy, forms of governance, and other real-world sources of power. But poetry has the capacity to empower us when all these other forces fail. Far from being a mere grace note in a sometimes heartless world, poetry can contribute in at least three ways to personal and social transformation:

- By helping us remember what it means to be human....

- By giving us the courage to walk a path with a heart....

- By inspiring us to take collective action toward meaningful social change....

Poetry has forever helped us remember what it means to be human. Surrounded as we always are by pressing short-term problems, we focus exclusively on solving them while ignoring those big, perplexing questions about the meaning of our lives. But if we ignore the big questions too long, life starts to lose its meaning. So from cave to cyberspace, we have chanted, sung, and written poetry to remind ourselves that short-term obsessions must never displace questions of ultimate concern.

Our obsession *du jour* in public education is making sure that our students pass high-stakes tests. If those tests truly measure mastery of significant subjects—a big "if" that is rarely addressed in the public debate about testing—helping students do well on them is not unimportant. But it cannot possibly be more important than offering the young an education that helps them find both personal meaning and ways to contribute to the common good.

Diverting most of our educational energies into test-taking rather than meaning-making is irresponsible, self-defeating, and ultimately tragic. Yet we are constantly drawn to those problems that have technical, or political, fixes rather than to the big questions that elude definitive answers. The ego and the intellect do not like to be baffled. They demand the smug self-satisfaction that comes from being able to say, "One more puzzle solved, and I'm the genius who solved it."

But poetry has a way of slipping past ego and intellect to speak directly to the heart about matters of great moment. And when the heart has received a message, we find it hard to turn away, even if the message engages us with issues that yield to no easy fix; if that were not the case, why would so many people still be working toward a world of truth, justice, and mercy?

To prove the power of poetry to penetrate the heart, we could cite classics late into the night. Think, for example, of T. S. Eliot's "Four Quartets," with its deep and nuanced insights into love and suffering, as witness these stanzas from the section titled "Little Gidding":

The dove descending breaks the air
With flame of incandescent terror
Of which the tongues declare
The one discharge from sin and error.
The only hope, or else despair
   Lies in the choice of pyre or pyre—
   To be redeemed from fire by fire.

Who then devised the torment? Love.
Love is the unfamiliar Name
Behind the hands that wove
The intolerable shirt of flame
Which human power cannot remove.
   We only live, only suspire
   Consumed by either fire or fire.

At the very least, these words offer perspective, reminding us that being stuck on the freeway, late for a date, with one's cell phone on the fritz, is not perhaps life's ultimate challenge. More to the point, they remind us that the love of anything worthy—like teaching and the lives of the young—will take us into the fire and must be pursued with fire.

But to test the power of poetry to get the heart's attention, let us play with a little poem of much less gravitas. Here is Ron Koertge's brief and witty "First Grade," a poem that, on the surface at least, seems intended largely to get a laugh:

Until then, every forest
had wolves in it, we thought
it would be fun to wear snowshoes
all the time, and we could talk to water.

So who is this woman with the gray
breath calling out names and pointing
to the little desks we will occupy
for the rest of our lives?

Read that poem one more time and watch how it goes to the heart. It takes us back to childhood, when we still had the precious gift of imagination. It helps us remember how precious a child's spirit is. It makes us sad by reminding us that schooling sometimes kills the spirit. It punctures our pretenses by portraying a teacher whose dedication is so devoid of humanity and humor that she exhales "gray breath," causing us to wonder, "Do I sometimes fill the room with the same deadly smog?" And the poem does all of this in just fifty-three simple words, less than half as many as this paragraph contains!

But "First Grade" can do more than remind us that imagination is a gift of the spirit and killing it off is a sin. Read that little poem with an open and vulnerable heart, and your "sad" might just morph into "mad." As we recover our dormant capacity for imagination, we realize that school does not have to be this way. In that realization is the energy of an anger that can lead us to protest the way education sometimes deforms children's lives—and to put our best efforts into creating schools where children can experience and explore the world's wonders and the power of ideas.

We live in a culture that fears anger and wants us to suppress it lest it become destructive. But anger, rightly placed, contains healing energy. Such anger wants to be used toward creative ends—and when we suppress it we end up depressed. What better way to protect the status quo than to convince people to tuck away their anger, leading them into a depression that deprives them of the will, the energy, and the hope for change?

It is no stretch to say that America is in a state of collective depression over the plight of our public schools. But the right poem, rightly read—whether silently and in solitude or, better yet, aloud and in community—can be an anti-depressant. Every time we take one we find a little more power to follow the imperatives of our hearts, no matter the risks.

Yet poetry can do more than empower individuals: it can energize communities of shared concern and action. Nowhere has this been more clearly revealed than in "The Words and Music of Social Change," an essay by psychiatrist Robert Coles.

Coles recounts his experience with the cadre of civil rights activists who gathered in Oxford, Ohio, in June 1964, to prepare for a nonviolent witness for racial justice called the Mississippi Summer Project. As the Ohio meeting got under way, news came that Mount Zion Church in Longdale, Mississippi—which was to have served as the site of a "Freedom School"—had been torched by the Ku Klux Klan.

In response, three young men—James Chaney, Andrew Goodman, and Michael Schwerner—decided to go to Mississippi early, ahead of the rest of the group. On June 21, 1964, all three were brutally beaten, then shot to death by Klansmen, including officers of the local sheriff's office, a case dramatized in the film *Mississippi Burning*.

It is easy to imagine the fear people must have felt when word of these murders got back to Ohio. As Robert Coles says, "Choices were there: to reconsider, to retreat, to 'regroup,' to wait and only later go south." But, he goes on, "Suddenly . . . something quite surprising and wonderful and (I can only use the word) awesome happened. Suddenly hundreds of young Americans became charged with new energy and determination. Suddenly I saw fear turn into toughness, vacillation into quiet conviction."

What propelled that group of largely privileged people from their safe haven in Ohio toward what were, at that moment, the killing grounds of Mississippi? It was not, says Robert Coles, social scientific information or theories of social change, as useful as those can be. Instead, people found the courage to act by singing folk songs; dancing together in circles; listening to the music of Beethoven, Brahms, and Berlioz; reciting the words of Shakespeare, Dostoyevsky, Thoreau, Tolstoy, and Auden; and reading Greek, Hebrew, and Christian texts.

It was poetry in its many guises that helped these ordinary people find the courage to walk into the fire, to take risky acts of conscience for which we honor them yet today.

Teaching with Fire

Serving the still-unfinished cause of racial and class justice is one of the many challenges we face in public education. Those challenges are daunting, but surely no more so than the dangers faced by those people gathered in Oxford, Ohio, in June 1964. Surely we, like they, can find in poetry reminders of what it means to be human, courage to walk a path with heart, and inspiration to take collective action toward meaningful change in the world of education.

The projects closest to the hearts of the authors of this Introduction—the "Courage to Teach" program of the Center for Courage & Renewal, and the "Small Schools" grants program of the Bill and Melinda Gates Foundation—share a common goal: to create humane and effective places for teachers, administrators, and students to work and to learn.

"Courage to Teach" seeks to renew the teacher's heart through retreats in which, among other things, we tap into the power of poetry read in community. "Small Schools" grants seek to create schools of human scale where students, teachers, and administrators together can weave authentic learning communities. And both projects seek to support a larger movement of people committed to reclaiming education as a search for purpose and meaning.

Such a search requires information and, yes, appropriate forms of assessment. But an education that fails to take us beyond mere information and testing into the struggle for personal and social change, is an education that fails our children, our society, and our world. We want schools that join mind and heart in imaginative and powerful ways, providing learning spaces where young people can wrestle with life's deepest questions, departing with an informed viewpoint and the capacity to act as moral agents. We want schools that, in the words of Deborah Meier, foster "feisty children."

To grow such children, we need educators who are alive and awake, who own and relish the most important work in the world, who understand what it means to "teach with fire." We need teachers and administrators who are listeners and learners, poets and storytellers, people who can draw out, lift up, lead, and follow. We need professionals who can move the debate about educational reform far beyond test scores toward a vision of human possibility.

We find hope in the growing ranks of feisty people who have the courage to teach. We find hope in the growing numbers of small, feisty schools that foster big ideas and help students and teachers come alive. As members of a public that owes a great debt of gratitude to such people and places, we want to offer them some of the sustenance they need, not only to survive but to serve as agents of change.

The words of the poets offer such sustenance, as do the words of the educators who have taken their poems to heart. May this book help pass the word, and the words, around.

Hearing the Call

*I*t is a serious matter to ask, Why do I teach? We don't come to teaching to punch the clock or count the dollars. Most of us come to teaching to answer a summons or bidding that commands us to do this work. We are drawn to teaching by our passion for our students and love of our subjects—and by our belief that connecting students to potent ideas will yield great things. We are drawn by a sense that we can make a difference in a child's life, in our world, and that engaging in such meaningful work will be cause for great personal fulfillment.

For this section, teachers shared poems and stories that remind them of their motives for becoming and continuing as teachers. Some remember with tenderness the mentors who evoked their passion to pursue this profession. Others describe how first encounters with teaching excited in them an insatiable desire to make this work their life. Others recognized that the summons to teach was not a choice but the best way to use their gifts.

Eight years ago, when I was considering giving up my job as a social worker, I tried to imagine what being a teacher would be like. I remember telling my wife, Sharon (a high school teacher), that I couldn't see myself working with small children in the classroom. Luckily, somewhere along the line, that changed.

Now I am a first-grade teacher. I sit in little chairs. I spend my days with children reading, writing, drawing, and playing guitar. I walk down hallways filled with children's art. I love my job. I can't imagine a better life.

Teaching first grade gives me many opportunities to share my love of poetry and music. First graders are natural poets and musicians. Reading and writing poetry together creates a solid bridge between my students and me. Music is a joyful common ground that equalizes as it unites.

I play guitar and sing with my students almost every day. My guitar is often my teaching partner. I turn to it when I need inspiration, comfort, and companionship. It helps me to focus, to clarify ideas, and to sort through emotions. It helps me to make music with my life, to polish the rough times into jewels, and it gives me strength to face the challenges I encounter in classroom life, "howlin like a guitar player."

—John J. Sweeney
First-Grade Teacher
Pennsylvania

Make Music with Your Life

Make music with your life
a
    jagged
silver tune
cuts every deepday madness
Into jewels   that you wear

Carry 16 bars of old blues
wit/you
everywhere you go
walk thru azure sadness
howlin
Like a guitar player

—*Bob O'Meally*

I first read "To be of use" at my mother's kitchen table a few weeks before starting my first teaching job. It made me feel proud and excited to be entering the teaching profession, and seemed a fitting send-off.

I had signed up for Teach for America and was set to move across the country to Oakland, California. I knew I was in for a challenge—I was going to teach with next to no training in a strange city—but I did not know how profound that challenge would be.

In September I found myself teaching math in a converted truancy center to sixty kids who had fallen (or been dropped) through the too-large cracks of the school district. The students were out of control, the staff inexperienced, and the administration unconcerned. I was miserable and my nervous determination turned to anxious doubt. How could I begin to teach?

The decision to leave my job, my first class of students, and my new identity as a teacher was one of the hardest I've had to make. I had come to "be of use" and instead found myself grossly underprepared in a situation that seemed hopeless.

A year later, this poem still serves as a guide as I prepare and search for work that is sustainable, work that feeds and keeps me afloat, even while I am submerged in it.

—Katya Levitan-Reiner
High School Math Substitute Teacher
California

To be of use

The people I love the best
jump into work head first
without dallying in the shallows
and swim off with sure strokes almost out of sight.
They seem to become natives of that element,
the black sleek heads of seals
bouncing like half-submerged balls.

I love people who harness themselves, an ox to a heavy cart,
who pull like water buffalo, with massive patience,
who strain in the mud and the muck to move things forward.
who do what has to be done, again and again.

I want to be with people who submerge
in the task, who go into the fields to harvest
and work in a row and pass the bags along,
who are not parlor generals and field deserters
but move in the common rhythm
when the food must come in or the fire be put out.

The work of the world is common as mud.
Botched, it smears the hands, crumbles to dust.
But the thing worth doing well done
has a shape that satisfies, clean and evident.
Greek amphoras for wine or oil,
Hopi vases that held corn, are put in museums
but you know they were made to be used.
The pitcher cries for water to carry
and a person for work that is real.

—Marge Piercy

Hearing the Call   5

Heather will not be in class today. The news was delivered with a whispered urgency. *She's been hospitalized, but tell no one. We're meeting at lunch.*

By the time we gathered, the word *suicide* was everywhere in the air, and not for the first time. Our work with these teens felt forever on the boundary of ecstasy and agony. We knew fury and suffering, the songs of despair, shards of hope sought always through a confusion. More than once I'd been awakened by an alarming phone call, gotten out of bed weak with the dawn.

This was not an attempt, we were told, but a gesture, a cry for help. The talk seemed both necessary and false. The calming clichés failed to soothe and the unmistakable subtext—walling the school off from fearful legal entanglements—was grating. Heather was never mentioned, referred to now only as *the situation.* The bleak system took center stage, the living, still-breathing girl kicked to the curb.

Later an older colleague, a literature teacher who was tiny and frail but with a makeup part fire, part steel, gave me a copy of "The Poet's Obligation." "This is for you," she said. "It describes your pathway and mine, and why you must stay with it."

—William Ayers

College Professor
Illinois

The Poet's Obligation

To whoever is not listening to the sea
this Friday morning, to whoever is cooped up
in house, office, factory or woman,
or street or mine or harsh prison cell:
to that person I come, and, without
    speaking or looking,
I arrive and open the door of the prison,
and a vibration starts up, vague and insistent,
a great roar of thunder sets in motion
the rumble of the planet and the foam,
the groaning rivers of the ocean rise,
the star vibrates swiftly in its corona,
and the sea beats, dies, and goes on beating.
So, drawn on by my destiny,
I ceaselessly must listen to and keep
the sea's lamenting in my consciousness
I must feel the crash of the hard water
and gather it up in a perpetual cup
so that, wherever those in prison may be,
wherever they suffer the autumn's castigation,
I may be present with an errant wave,
I move in and out of windows,
and hearing me, eyes may lift themselves
saying "How can I reach the sea?"

And I shall broadcast, saying nothing,
the starry echoes of the wave,
a breaking up of foam and of quicksand,
a rustling of salt withdrawing,
the grey cry of sea-birds on the coast.
So, through me, freedom and the sea
Will call in answer to the shrouded heart.

—*Pablo Neruda*

I read "I pastori" aloud at my grandmother's funeral. It seemed a fitting tribute to Nonna, my Italian grandmother. My earliest connection to poetry was at her knee. Oh, how I loved being bounced up and down on Nonna's lap while she recited Italian nursery rhymes and poems and beckoned me playfully to join her in recitation. But even more than that, "I pastori" honors my grandmother's immigrant history. It is a poem about journeys, sustenance, relationships, renewal, and tradition, and it is set in Abruzzi, my Nonna's birthplace. Reading this poem aloud in celebration of Nonna's life gave me great comfort. It also inspired me to carry on in my grandmother's memory.

My grandmother was proud, she was strong, and she was courageous. She valued education. She taught herself to read English and delighted in the academic accomplishments of her grandchildren. She encouraged me when I told her I wanted to be a teacher; she told me there was no finer or nobler profession.

"I pastori," taped to the wall by my desk, serves as my staff. It grounds me and supports me in my work with student teachers and teachers: *September, let us go. It is time to migrate.* Teaching is a journey, and not unlike the one experienced by the shepherds in d'Annunzio's poem, it can be challenging and arduous; but ultimately, teaching is a journey of hope, promise, and fulfillment. Grazie, Nonna.

—Susan Etheredge
College Professor
Massachusetts

I pastori (The Shepherds)

September, let us go. It is time to migrate.
Now in the land of the Abruzzi my shepherds
leave the pens and go towards the sea:
they go down to the wild Adriatic
which is green like the mountain pastures.

They have drunk deep at alpine springs,
so that the taste of native water
may remain in exile hearts as a comfort,
to charm their thirst for long upon the way.
They have renewed their staffs of hazel.

And they go along the ancient drove-path to the plain,
as if by a grassy, silent river,
upon the traces of the early fathers.
O voice of him who first
knows the trembling of the sea!

Now on the shore at its side marches
the flock. The air is without motion.
The sun so gilds the living wool
that it hardly differs from the sand.
Sea-washing, trampling, sweet sounds.

Ah why am I not with my shepherds?

—*Gabriele D'Annunzio*

During my adolescence, words began to resonate with a different kind of energy for me. I remember hearing the words, "Judy, Mama died." These words penetrated my soul like a devastating tornado, uprooting everything in its path, twisting uncontrollably in whatever direction it wanted to with no regard for humanity.

When the interment was final, my mother's body was committed to the ground. Seeing the deep hole that seemed so dark and cold, I felt confused and lonely. The following week, I returned to my junior high school. It became my new refuge. While sitting and daydreaming in my seventh-grade English class, I reluctantly picked up my assigned reading text and began flipping through the pages, starting from the back, to the front. This is where I first met Emily Dickinson. I heard her voice as I read the words from her poem "The Chariot." She allowed me to conceptualize the beauty that came with death. It was at this precise moment that I fully understood that it wasn't my mother's fault that she had to die, but it was death himself who had come and taken her without permission.

From that day forward, I made up my mind that I wouldn't be angry; instead I would do something to make my mother proud of me even though I knew she would no longer be in my life physically.

I became a schoolteacher.

—Judy R. Smith
Special Education Teacher
Pennsylvania

The Chariot

Because I could not stop for Death –
He kindly stopped for me –
The Carriage held but just Ourselves –
And Immortality.

We slowly drove – He knew no haste
And I had put away
My labor and my leisure too,
For His Civility –

We passed the School, where Children strove
At Recess – in the Ring –
We passed the Fields of Gazing Grain –
We passed the Setting Sun –

Or rather – He passed Us –
The Dews drew quivering and chill –
For only Gossamer, my Gown –
My Tippet – only Tulle –

We paused before a House that seemed
A Swelling of the Ground –
The Roof was scarcely visible –
The Cornice – in the Ground –

Since then – 'tis Centuries – and yet
Feels shorter than the Day
I first surmised the Horses' Heads
Were toward Eternity –

—*Emily Dickinson*

Teaching chose me. I wanted to be a lawyer, but my brother decided to become a doctor—and in 1950, free tuition at Buffalo State worked best with the family budget. A few weeks into college I knew I was born to teach. I taught in California, I taught in Omaha, and I taught in rural Nebraska. Long summer vacations were perfect for a mother of five children, two of whom I taught in my twenty-one years in the classroom.

Children came to me as second graders, as fourth graders, as fifth and sixth graders. A thousand or more hours later they moved up and onward. I retired (how quickly the time goes) ten years ago. I am asked how many of the children I remember. I remember all of them.

My mother died a few years ago, at the age of ninety-three. At her request the priest read Tennyson's "Crossing the Bar" at her funeral. As I listened to the words, I remembered Bill, who was murdered in Texas the year after I taught him in sixth grade; Brian, who died in a car accident just after high school graduation; and Catherine, who struggled with a brain tumor in second grade.

As teachers we feel the children in our classrooms become part of our lives. We witness them growing, learning, and becoming. Sometimes we witness and experience their tragedies as well. Somehow Tennyson's words make those losses easier to bear.

—Marj Vandenack

Retired Elementary School Teacher
Nebraska

Crossing the Bar

Sunset and evening star,
    And one clear call for me!
And may there be no moaning of the bar,
    When I put out to sea,

But such a tide as moving seems asleep,
    Too full for sound and foam,
When that which drew from out the boundless deep
    Turns again home.

Twilight and evening bell,
    And after that the dark!
And may there be no sadness of farewell,
    When I embark;

For tho' from out our bourne of Time and Place
    The flood may bear me far,
I hope to see my Pilot face to face
    When I have crost the bar.

—Alfred, Lord Tennyson

I know about hanging on to threads. Twenty-three years ago I was on the verge of becoming a teacher when my husband's grandmother's farm came up for sale. I dropped out of graduate school to help purchase the land. Since then I have been a teacher to my three children and an active volunteer in their schools. I have taught oboe, led the Cub Scouts, and hayed the fields. Through it all, my desire to teach has never diminished.

As an undergraduate studying at the University of Washington under Nelson Bentley, the themes from poetry of staying true to one's dreams were a good match to my personal philosophy. William Stafford's poem speaks directly to this.

Many people can't see what is guiding me. They wonder why I continue to go for a degree even as age creeps up and people around me are changing. But the thread keeps me on track. It is a combination of wanting to emulate excellent teachers I had and wanting to help children be the best people they can be. It is about effecting change in our world in the face of hopelessness.

I am currently student teaching in middle school English classes as I pursue a master's degree through City University in Vancouver, Washington. In this program many of my fellow students are also hanging on to a thread, pursuing the calling to become a teacher. Hopefully we won't ever let go of that thread.

—*Lisa Drumheller Sudar*
Student Teacher
Washington

The Way It Is

There's a thread you follow. It goes among
things that change. But it doesn't change.
People wonder about what you are pursuing.
You have to explain about the thread.
But it is hard for others to see.
While you hold it you can't get lost.
Tragedies happen; people get hurt
or die; and you suffer and get old.
Nothing you do can stop time's unfolding.
You don't ever let go of the thread.

—*William Stafford*

Walt Whitman's picture makes him appear wise and haughty. He seems to know that I need a specific directive like, "This is what you shall do." Fatherly advice.

I get so easily tangled in the daily details of teaching. Usually it is in frustration or exhaustion that I finally look up at the lines on his weathered face and the lines of the passage and remind myself I cannot remember a stitch of content from my tenth-grade year. Nothing from freshman English or junior history. What I do remember is what a success felt like or when I brushed against self-awareness because of solid and dedicated adults. To "re-examine all you have been told" is really the lesson that matters most to my students and to myself.

I share Whitman's words with my juniors each year, make them cards to stick into their notebooks and carry around with them. Many keep the cards visible the rest of the year. Their reminders. To think that our lives could be described as a "great poem" pushes me out the door each day to write the next line.

—Lori Douglas

High School English Teacher
Washington

From Preface to *Leaves of Grass*

Love the earth and sun and the animals, despise riches, give alms to
everyone that asks, stand up for the stupid and crazy, devote your income
and labor to others, hate tyrants, argue not concerning God, have patience
and indulgence toward the people, take off your hat to nothing known
or unknown or to any man or number of men, go freely with powerful
uneducated persons and with the young and the mothers of families,
read these leaves in the open air every season of every year of your life,
re-examine all you have been told at school or church or in any book,
dismiss whatever insults your own soul and your very flesh shall be a
great poem.

—*Walt Whitman*

I don't remember the first time I read "Dream Deferred," but it stays with me as a warning to pay attention to the dreams around us, our own and everyone else's. This poem is why I am in the public school business.

When I became a teacher it was not really to teach. I just wanted to help kids stay out of trouble. During a college internship with the Department of Juvenile Justice in New York City, I learned that the juvenile justice system would be a hard place from which to do that. I became a teacher out of fear—fear of what happened to kids who ended up in jail, kids whose dreams were drying up, festering, and even exploding.

It was clear that all my students had dreams. I sought to nurture those dreams—linking them to role models in their lives, in history, and even in fiction so they could see for themselves that their dreams are attainable and so they would be inspired to realize those dreams.

I am still in public education and I am still motivated by this poem. While I have become passionate about teaching and learning for its own sake (not only to keep kids out of trouble), I am, to be honest, still afraid that too many dreams may be deferred. This fear keeps me doing what I do.

—Heather Kirkpatrick

Director of Secondary Education, Aspire Public Schools
California

Dream Deferred

What happens to a dream deferred?

Does it dry up
like a raisin in the sun?

Or fester like a sore—
And then run?

Does it stink like rotten meat?
Or crust and sugar over—
like a syrupy sweet?

Maybe it just sags
like a heavy load.

Or does it explode?

—*Langston Hughes*

When I first heard Marian read this prayer, I was struck by the way "I care and I'm willing to serve" resounded with my life. I have always considered it a great blessing that my occupation and my vocation have coincided; that my professional life has been my calling. Over my three decades in public education, I have always found inspiration in my concern for the welfare of children. And though I have worn many hats, I have always considered myself first and foremost a servant-leader.

This poem is particularly inspiring because it reminds us that we often sell ourselves short in terms of the unique contribution we can each make to the world. Wayne Muller helped me understand the difference between talents and gifts when he said that talents are things we can teach others, but gifts are uniquely for us to do. It might be something small like telling someone of our love or something big like starting a program. But our gift to the world is to do that one thing we have been called upon to do. And so, although we might not have the talents of others, that shouldn't stop us from responding to our inner calling and desire to serve.

The balance of the inner and outer life is allowing the caring on the inside to be expressed in the service on the outside. As Marian has said, "Service is the rent you pay for living."

—Linda Lantieri

Director, Project Renewal of Educators for Social Responsibility
New York

I Care and I'm Willing to Serve

Lord, I can't preach like Dr. Martin Luther King Jr. or Jesse Jackson or turn a poetic phrase like Maya Angelou, but I care, and I'm willing to serve, and to use what talents I have to build a world of peace.

I don't have Fred Shuttlesworth's and Harriet Tubman's courage or Andy Young's political skills, but I care, and I'm willing to serve.

I can't sing like Fannie Lou Hamer or organize like Ella Baker, Bayard Rustin, or John Dear, but I care, and I'm willing to serve.

I'm not holy like Archbishop Tutu, forgiving like Mandela, or disciplined like Gandhi, but I care and I'm willing to serve and to fight in a nonviolent manner.

I'm not brilliant like Dr. Du Bois or Elizabeth Cady Stanton or as eloquent as Sojourner Truth and Booker T. Washington, but I care and I'm willing to serve.

I don't have Mother Teresa's saintliness, Dorothy Day's love, or Cesar Chavez's gentle, tough spirit, but I care and I'm willing to serve.

God, it's not as easy as the Sixties to frame an issue and forge a solution, but I care and I'm willing to serve.

My mind and body are not as swift as in youth, and my energy comes in spurts but I care, and I'm willing to serve.

I'm so young nobody will listen, I'm not sure what to say or do, but I care and I'm willing to serve.

I can't see or hear well, speak good English, stutter sometimes, and get real scared, and I really hate risking criticism, but I care and I'm willing to serve.

Use me as Thou wilt to save Thy Children today and tomorrow, and to build a nation and a world to where no child is left behind, and every child is loved and every child is safe.

—*Marian Wright Edelman*

Cherishing the Work

There is much that is sacred in our work. Much that is worthy of reverence and awe. Much that we love and cherish. The irrepressible surge of joy that comes from a class well taught, the miraculous sense of wonder that comes from witnessing students making sense of their world, the powerful esprit that comes from working with colleagues and parents to create a space where learning is honored and children thrive—these are the subjects of many poems in this section.

Other poems remind us that as adults we inhabit a different world than we did as children. Our stance, our fears, our joys, and the sensibilities that guide our encounters with the world have shifted in shape and intensity since we strode the world as children and students. Children's book writer Edith Nesbit said that when she was a child she used to "pray fervently, tearfully, that when she should grow up she might never forget what she thought, felt, and suffered as a child." These poems invite us to retrieve the fragile memories of childhood so we can work with more heart and wisdom as adults.

When life is unquiet or even in total disarray, I retreat to my favorite bookshop or library. On one such excursion, I encountered "First Reader." I made a quick connection, remembering the protagonists who had been so important in my own process of becoming a reader. But I trembled slightly as I read the last line, "we were forgetting how to look, learning how to read."

Once I dreamed of being the catalyst that would bring my students the joy and serenity I have found in becoming lost in a book. Now, as a teacher, I have taken a step beyond that.

I teach children whose lives have been largely untouched by books and whose backgrounds are amazingly diverse. They have learned to look at the world through lenses I have not. I must alter my own purpose so that I honor their ways of looking and so that nothing is lost in the process of becoming schooled.

This poem is pasted into my reading notebook; it is the first thing I see before deciding what I want to teach next. It is my way of remembering that the diverse experiences and backgrounds of the children I teach are newfound gold. My task is to ensure that all these children find ways of preserving and sharing their special ways of looking while at the same time discovering how to look with other eyes. That is the joy of being a reader.

—Sandra Dean
Primary and Preschool Teacher
California

First Reader

I can see them standing politely on the wide pages
that I was still learning to turn,
Jane in a blue jumper, Dick with his crayon-brown hair,
playing with a ball or exploring the cosmos
of the backyard, unaware they are the first characters,
the boy and girl who begin fiction.

Beyond the simple illustration of their neighborhood
the other protagonists were waiting in a huddle:
frightening Heathcliff, frightened Pip, Nick Adams
carrying a fishing rod. Emma Bovary riding into Rouen.

But I would read about the perfect boy and his sister
even before I would read about Adam and Eve, garden and gate,
and before I heard the name Gutenberg, the type
of their simple talk was moving into my focusing eyes.

It was always Saturday and he and she
were always pointing at something and shouting "Look!"
pointing at the dog, the bicycle, or at their father
as he pushed a hand mower over the lawn,
waving at aproned mother framed in the kitchen doorway,
pointing toward the sky, pointing at each other.

They wanted us to look but we had looked already
and seen the shaded lawn, the wagon, the postman.
We had seen the dog, walked, watered and fed the animal,
and now it was time to discover the infinite, clicking
permutations of the alphabet's small and capital letters.
Alphabetical ourselves in the rows of classroom desks,
we were forgetting how to look, learning how to read.

—*Billy Collins*

I arrived late to the teaching profession. Before teaching, I worked in and around theater. I never imagined myself becoming a teacher. But when my father died, and with some good mentoring, I began to reexamine my choices, which led me to teaching.

After fifteen years of teaching in New York City, I still wonder how I got so lucky. Had I remained in the theater, I might have had regrets. Teaching meant assuming a very different role. I joined the "parental generation" in that way, with the responsibility that it implies. That's quite different from the life of a sometime actor, waiter, temp worker, and sales clerk. Looking at fifteen years of teaching, even the "bad" times were very well spent.

The particular cultural role I inhabit in my profession is always on my mind. I am both a "model and tool" for my students, offering building blocks of knowledge, skills, and values that they will assemble as they see fit.

I do not remember precisely what my teachers taught me in grade school, but I remember the relationships I had with them and their individual characters. I have chosen to use some of them as my *axe handles,* "for the model is indeed near at hand" and I am keenly aware that I carry the same responsibility to those I teach. I must pass on a model that they can shape. That is, in the end, as Snyder says, "How we go on."

—Curtis Borg
Special Education Middle School Teacher
New York

Axe Handles

One afternoon the last week in April
Showing Kai how to throw a hatchet
One-half turn and it sticks in a stump.
He recalls the hatchet-head
Without a handle, in the shop
And go gets it, and wants it for his own.
A broken-off axe handle behind the door
Is long enough for a hatchet,
We cut it to length and take it
With the hatchet head
And working hatchet, to the wood block.
There I begin to shape the old handle
With the hatchet, and the phrase
First learned from Ezra Pound
Rings in my ears!
"When making an axe handle
    the pattern is not far off."
And I say this to Kai
"Look: We'll shape the handle
By checking the handle
Of the axe we cut with—"
And he sees. And I hear it again:
It's in Lu Ji's *Wên Fu*, fourth century
A.D. "Essay on Literature"—in the
Preface: "In making the handle
Of an axe
By cutting wood with an axe
The model is indeed near at hand."

My teacher Shih-hsiang Chen
Translated that and taught it years ago
And I see: Pound was an axe,
Chen was an axe, I am an axe
And my son a handle, soon
To be shaping again, model
And tool, craft of culture,
How we go on.

—*Gary Snyder*

On a gray afternoon, as daylight and my vision for teaching and learning with children were fading, a wise friend slid David Whyte's *The House of Belonging* across the coffee table. The book fell open to this poem and I instantly recognized in the words a reminder of the gifts we bring to each other in education.

"Working Together" reminds me that sometimes my plans and expectations are less important than supporting a child deeply engaged in discovery. It is something unexplainable and quite miraculous. As six-year-old David told his mom after his first week in our classroom, "You know that's an easy place to be good." It is pure gift to realize that children are finding the true shape of their own self within an inviting learning community.

Believing in this synergy, I come to children with a deeper trust in their unique learning patterns, as well as my own growth. I can step back and breathe in the wonder of confusion—mine or a child's own, crossing bridges between home and school, self and other, the familiar and the unknown. It is as easy to feel lost when facing change as it is to know the joy of anticipation. Every passage requires letting go of what has become precious and opening to treasures that are waiting to be gathered. During these moments there is no separation between us, only recognition for the gifts we share in our journey to be true to ourselves and open to life.

—Jani Barker
First-Grade Teacher
Oregon

Working Together

We shape our self
to fit this world

and by the world
are shaped again.

The visible
and the invisible

working together
in common cause,

to produce
the miraculous.

I am thinking of the way
the intangible air

passed at speed
round a shaped wing

easily
holds our weight.

So may we, in this life
trust

to those elements
we have yet to see

or imagine,
and look for the true

shape of our own self,
by forming it well

to the great
intangibles about us.

—*David Whyte*

Before I could stand, my parents began instilling in me a love of nature. Sitting on my mother's lap by a lake in the Pine Barrens of New Jersey, riding on my father's back up a trail through fragrant forests in Maine, or splashing about in warm tide pools with my siblings in coastal South Carolina, I was connecting my heart, mind, and senses to the world around me. As I grew, we continued to hike, camp, and explore as a family. I was proud to be the kid whose mom would hold a horseshoe crab, garter snake, or daddy longlegs in her bare hands for us to marvel at!

Passing this awareness along to children is a passion of mine. Often poetry is the starting place—especially when preparing in the classroom for an outdoor adventure. "Fueled" was particularly helpful when I was teaching girls at a private school, many of whom had material things but little acquaintance with dirt, rocks, or critters. I wanted the outing to make a meaningful, lasting impression on them. We discussed the poem, memorized it, and vowed to celebrate whatever "springtime miracles" we found.

That day was magical. We clapped and cheered for tiny seedlings, patted crayfish on their backs, sketched May apples, and met insects eye to eye. Later, the girls' reflections emerged as expressive poetry, beautiful pictures, poignant journal entries, and thank-you messages to me that confirmed I had indeed accomplished my mission!

—Betsy Motten
Fourth-Grade Teacher
Pennsylvania

Fueled

Fueled
by a million
man-made
wings of fire—
the rocket tore a tunnel
through the sky—
and everybody cheered.
Fueled
only by a thought from God—
the seedling
urged its way
through thicknesses of black—
and as it pierced
the heavy ceiling of the soil—
and launched itself
up into outer space—
no
one
even
clapped.

—*Marcie Hans*

I chose "The Red Wheelbarrow" for its grip on real life. I'd been teaching poetry to classes of seven- to nine-year-old boys with severe emotional disturbances. As writer-in-residence, I try to expose students to literature and teach them to write from a writer's perspective; these boys wanted no part of it. Many of them were on medication, few came from stable homes, about half were in foster care. They couldn't sit through any forty-five-minute class, let alone one on poetry.

Williams believed it was the poet's prerogative to collect objects, examine them, and write them down. I wanted my students to do the same. These kids had plenty of material. Their lives were so "real" they often had trouble managing them. Before my students could describe a toy the way Williams had described the wheelbarrow, they had to understand the poem.

They didn't. We read it a few times. The students stared at me blankly. It dawned on me: this was the South Bronx; they had no idea what a wheelbarrow was. I drew one on the board—still nothing. Then I remembered the game where one person holds another's legs and drives them like a wheelbarrow.

We went out in the hall, and the students raced against each other. They were ecstatic. I'd never seen them so happy. They would have done anything for one more race in the hallway, but they'd promised to write. Sweating and panting, they took out their pencils.

—Sarah Fay

Artist in Residence, Teachers and Writers Collaborative
New York

The Red Wheelbarrow

so much depends
upon

a red wheel
barrow

glazed with rain
water

beside the white
chickens.

—*William Carlos Williams*

I love when my students revel in words, rubbing them together and exploring the impact of language in our lives. Jumbling words, language, and art together can be joyful work. We even use slang, try out new phrases, and discover ways of saying the same old words. I find that my students (including those who are struggling with acquiring language) have so much success during our word play that it encourages them to increase participation in class assignments.

I reread "Poem Against the First Grade" each year, reminding me to view students as individuals who have the ability to experience "unbroken joy with words," and for me to avoid becoming a proper sad giant "armed to the ears with pencils and rules." Yes, we do other writing activities like formal writing, editing, and writing-on-demand. But those activities are not what make the memories.

Each year I strive to cultivate the love of words. I want my students "Thumping the pano keys like a mudpie chef, [who] goes wild with words." Students arrive, enthusiastic learners ready to explore their world. But something happens in our educational system. Beginning in first grade (sometimes earlier), we pour them into easy-to-assess molds, and despair when we no longer hear their creative voices as these "molds" harden into adolescence. Venn's poem remains with me as a constant reminder to savor the play of language and to encourage "joyful error."

—Theresa Gill

Middle School Teacher
California

Poem Against the First Grade

Alex, my son, with backberry jam
smeared ear to ear and laughing,
rides his unbroken joy with words
so fast we let him get away
on the jamjar without clean cheeks first.

He spills frasasass
tea with milk and honey;
a red-chafted schlicker
beats our cottonwood drum.
Thumping the pano keys
like a mudpie chef,
he goes wild with words
at the wittle wooden
arms inside, a hundred
Pinoschios to singsong.
If he can't wide byebye
bike to the candy store,
where he is Master Rich
with one penny, words turn
to tears in his mouf. Once
in a while, he walks home
with pumpumpumpernickel bread,
his nose twitching so fast
a wabbit would love him.

Now this language isn't taught in first grade.
Alicia, his tister, knows this *fact*.
Be he juggles it around all day
until she makes him spit it out like
a catseye marble or a tack. "Ax," she says,
"that's not *right*." She's been among giants
who wipe off the dialect of backberry jam,
then pour hot wax on each bright mistake.

I hope for a bad seal on Ax and tister,
encourage the mold of joyous error
that proper sad giants, armed to the ears
with pencils and rules, all forgot.

—*George Venn*

I first met this poem on Victoria Dallas-Stevenson's classroom door at The Lab School in the Bronx. I have seen many front door welcoming messages, but none caught my teacher's heart more than this one. To me it captures the essence of what childhood and education can be at their very best—full of infinite possibilities, exploration, imagination, and enchantment. It speaks directly to the love of learning and to the sense of wonder we try to instill and encourage in all our students.

When I left The Lab School, I made sure to take the poem with me and hang it on my new classroom door. I am now in my fifth year teaching fourth grade at P.S. 198, an urban school with an almost exclusively minority and underresourced population. I am committed to these students and believe that giving them a chance to succeed is one of the most important jobs there is.

I mean to send a powerful message to my students when they first walk through my door. The poem says to them that no matter where you come from, who you've been, or what you've seen, when you enter my room everything is possible.

After our year together, when my students walk out of my classroom for the last time, and beyond the school's door in the Bronx, I hope they feel like they can "sail tall ships, And fly where the wind has flown."

—Lamson T. Lam
Elementary School Teacher
New York

On the Other Side of the Door

On the other side of the door
I can be a different me,
As smart and as brave and as funny or strong
As a person could want to be.
There's nothing too hard for me to do,
There's no place I can't explore
Because everything can happen
On the other side of the door.

On the other side of the door
I don't have to go alone.
If you come, too, we can sail tall ships
And fly where the wind has flown.
And wherever we go, it is almost sure
We'll find what we're looking for
Because everything can happen
On the other side of the door.

—Jeff Moss

"You can do whatever you want. I will support you in everything. Always." The last line of this poem speaks of the power of family love and support, especially in families such as was mine, that had limited material resources to give.

In 1966, when I started teaching, few books discussed the education of Puerto Rican students in the United States—none written or edited by a Puerto Rican. When I decided to write *Puerto Rican Students in U.S. Schools,* I called on Lydia Cortés (my sister and a gifted poet) to write the opening piece.

I cried when I read her poem. It continues to evoke strong emotions in me. I too had my share of demeaning, disparaging, and uncaring teachers. I also remember those who made a difference. Mrs. Phillips, my fifth-grade teacher and the only African American teacher I had until I was a doctoral student, caught me cheating and gave me the only zero I ever received—and I knew it was because she believed in me. And Mr. and Mrs. Fried, high school French teachers, who made me proud that I spoke Spanish and showed me that knowing one language can help with a new one.

"I Remember" reflects the reality of school for many children. It is about children's resiliency and the power of family to counteract negative messages of schools and society. Most of all it is a tribute to teachers who make a difference.

—*Sonia Nieto*

College Professor
Massachusetts

I Remember

I remember kindergarten
I remember having to say good-bye to Mami
I remember crying
I remember not understanding the teacher
I remember the English lessons with pretty Miss
    Powell
who made the boxy words fit just right in my
    mouth without pain
I remember the teachers who said, "You don't
    look Puerto Rican,"
expecting to hear me say thank you very much
I remember overhearing some saying Puerto Ricans
don't care about their children, Puerto Ricans
    aren't clean
I remember the heat of shame rising up,
    changing the color of my face
I remember praying no one heard what the
    teachers said, praying
no one see my hurt red as a broken heart
I remember Mr. Seidman in the 4th grade and
    how he chose
me for a big part in the school play
I remember feeling important
I remember memorizing all those lines and
    Mami helping me
I remember both Mr. Seidman and Mami
    smiling, proud—
looking at me!—the night of the performance
I remember making the audience laugh and the
    applause
I remember moving to Flatbush from Fort
    Greene—

from a fifth floor walk-up to our very own house
I remember going from Girl's High to Erasmus
    Hall
I remember going from smart to borderline in
    one day
I remember the bio teacher, Miss Nash, calling
    me stupid
because I didn't know how to use a microscope
I remember Mr. and Mrs. Hamberger
I remember how I laughed when I heard I was
    getting
one for political science and the other for
    economics
I remember being amazed when they made
    learning a wonder-filled adventure
I remember working hard for them both and
    the faith each had in me
I remember the A's I got in their classes
I remember being Puerto Rican in Erasmus Hall
    High School
because I was the only one—until my sister
    followed—on the academic track
I remember the guidance counselor advising me
    to be
a bilingual secretary because I certainly was not
    college material
I remember Papi, with his third grade
    education, saying,
"Lidín, tú puedes hacer lo que quieres. Yo te
    apoyo en todo. Siempre."

—*Lydia Cortés*

Some poems stick with you on your journey through life. I recited this poem as part of my high school valedictory address in 1986. I chose it for my intimate class of seventy-three because of the many places we'd figuratively traveled as a class. From retreats to parties and proms, we celebrated rich friendships. And when one of our beloved classmates was tragically killed, we embraced one another in the spirit of the Christian Brothers' education. "Nothing gold can stay" synthesized the complexities of our four years together, and how we emerged as a product of our nurturing environment at St. Mary's.

As founding principal of a new urban charter high school, I now try and recreate the nurturing environment that served me so well at St. Mary's. As principal, I am surrounded by budding souls for whom life seems rich and bursting with opportunity. But keeping this sense of fresh authenticity is a challenge. Although you want it to last forever, you begin to see signs of change. This is the essence of high school. Just when it is becoming most enjoyable and comfortable, it's time to move on.

When I reflect on Frost's words, I am reminded that any given time in your life is but a season. Just like the fall of mankind of which Frost so giftedly reminds us, you never really appreciate the Garden of Eden until dawn goes down to day, realizing that nothing gold can stay.

—Troyvoi Hicks

High School Principal
California

Nothing Gold Can Stay

Nature's first green is gold,
Her hardest hue to hold.
Her early leaf's a flower;
But only so an hour.
Then leaf subsides to leaf.
So Eden sank to grief,
So dawn goes down to day.
Nothing gold can stay.

—*Robert Frost*

Rogelio, Robin, Leticia, Terry, Frank, and other students of mine at Palo Alto College in Texas swirl into focus. Serious students who might be caring for a dying mother, managing a large family as a single parent, trying to become someone after a jail stint, undergoing cancer treatment, holding down two jobs. Still, they persevere.

I recall driving to West Virginia to interview Rae Ellen McKee, the 1991 Teacher of the Year, who told me that her father was her role model, the teacher she wanted to become. During her childhood she watched him as principal and teacher nurture children and their families outside the classroom. He worked "under the table" to give kids lunch who would have gone without. He "hauled people to the doctor," and always had someone extra staying at their home. Sometimes he would go out late at night and quietly put needed items on porches or at doors for people who would not take charity. That's what she saw as the teacher's calling. The classroom was almost an attachment to the real work.

This poem surely is the proof that we must love our work and consider our students as whole persons, not merely as names on the roll book or roster. I honor and emulate this poem's teacher, who can look beyond and understand the student who sometimes sleeps in his class. A teacher who is aware as all teachers must be.

—Ellen Shull
College Professor
Texas

The Mouse

Tyrone is a junior in my creative writing class
during the day. After school, in order to support
his family & Tyrone Junior, he puts on his costume
& becomes the giant Chuck-E-Cheese Mouse.

He likes this job, likes to stroll around the restaurant
wearing the big mouse head, talking to the little kids,
making them laugh, but once in a while, he says,
one gets scared & cries, so he scurries off to another table.

Often Tyrone, a heavy set black fellow, will fall asleep
in class, his head on the desk. Sometimes he even snores.
Today, however, he is alert, teeters way back in his chair,
smiles largely, and happily flirts with the girls in the class.

I begin to explain that sometimes poetry doesn't strike
us solely at the cerebral level, that we respond to it in a more
intuitive way—to its music, its nuance, its cadence & sound—
or to its shape on the page, the white negative space.

For instance, I continue, *here is my very favorite line of poetry
from Wallace Stevens—"They who left the flame freaked sun
to seek a sun of fuller fire." I have absolutely no idea at all
as to what this line means, but it thrills me each time I hear it.*

Tyrone leans back further in his chair until it touches the wall,
smiles his handsome know-it-all smile, and says, *Shit, man, I knows
what that mean. These peoples, they be at a really good party,
but they just gets up & leaves to go to a much cooler party.*

I'm about to laugh at the simple mindedness of this—
his facile interpretation of the Stevens' line that had for twenty
years enchanted and baffled me—when I realize how right he is,
this cheerful and mannish boy who was already a father—

a father who for his son each night becomes the mouse.

—*Gary Blankenburg*

On my first day teaching English in a small Vermont town, I was explaining an introductory assignment when Shane, a round, freckle-faced kid wearing a NASCAR T-shirt, asked, "Mr. Mindich, when you say poem, do you mean something like: Here I sit broken hearted, pulled my pants down but only—" Unfortunately (or fortunately), he began giggling uncontrollably and couldn't finish.

As other, more polished kids wondered what to make of this, I said, "Absolutely."

Not that school should be one big bathroom joke, but the goofy joy in Shane's face at that moment typifies what I love about teaching and how I try to teach poetry.

Too often we focus on dour, inaccessible texts that give kids a pigeonholed view of poetry. What I love about "Sunday, Tarzan in His Hammock" is that Buzbee manages to write with interesting poetic images and still give a hysterical twist on the normally heroic Tarzan.

Yes, the poem does push boundaries with Tarzan's voyeurism and the use of "fuck it," but those elements serve to make his character more ironic and show kids that good poetry doesn't have to be stiff.

Buzbee's piece has inspired my high school students to write poems on topics ranging from the fears of G.I. Joe to the heroism of the lonely kid in the lunchroom. But I also read "Tarzan" now and then to remind myself of moments like Shane's recital and the way I want my classroom to be.

—Dan Mindich

High School English Teacher
Hawaii

Sunday, Tarzan in His Hammock

When the king of the jungle first wakes up, he
    thinks
it's going to be a great day, as laden with
    possibility
as the banana tree with banana hands, but by ten
he's still in the hammock, arms and legs dull as
termite mounds. He stares at the thatched roof
    and realizes
that his early good mood was a leftover from
    Saturday,
when he got so much done: a great day, he
    saved
the tiger cub trapped in the banyan, herded the
    hippos
away from the tourists and their cameras and
    guns,
restrung and greased the N-NW vines, and all
    by noon.
All day he went about his duties, not so much
    kingly duties
as custodial, and last night, he and Cheetah
    went for a walk
under the ostrich-egg moon. This morning
    nothing stirs him.
The world is a stagnant river, a scummy creek's
    dammed pool.
Cheetah's gone chattering off, Jane is in town,
and the rest of the animals are busy with one
    another—
fighting, eating, mating. Tarzan can barely
    move,

he does not want to move. Does the gazelle
    ever feel this
lassitude, does it ever want to lie down and just
    stare,
no longer caring for its own safety, tired of the
    vigilance?
Does the lion, fat in the grass, ever think, fuck
    it,
let the wounded springbok live, who cares?
Tarzan thinks maybe he'll go to the bathing
    pools
and watch the village girls bathe, splashing in
    the sun,
their breasts and thighs perfect. He wishes
    someone
would bring him a gourd of palm wine, a platter
    of
imported fruits—kiwi, jack fruit, star fruit—
or maybe a bowl of roasted yams slathered in
    goat butter.
Maybe Jane will bring him a book.
He hears far off in the dense canopy a zebra's
    cry for help,
those damned jackals again, but, no, he will not
    move.
Let the world take care of itself, let the world
    eat
the world. He can live without the call of the
    wild.
He thinks.

—Lewis Buzbee

On The Edge

*M*ake no mistake, teaching is high-stakes work. What happens in our classrooms matters. Futures are born, dreams emboldened, passions ignited—or not. Because it matters, we need to be alive in this work.

When we are scared, ground down, and lonely, we cannot do and be our best. Teachers know fear. Standing before a classroom of students is a daily exercise in vulnerability. Our students can defy us, disregard us, or reject what we offer. When we feel vulnerable and fearful, we either hunker down in isolation or strike out against that which threatens us. Neither approach imbues the world with beauty and heart.

In this section, teachers describe how poems stir them to name and face that which depletes their hearts: the fear of not doing enough, the shame of being inadequate, the fear that our students need more than we can give. Daily these teachers encounter situations that push them to the edge; daily they call upon rare and beautiful resolve—often found or supported by poetry—because they know that what happens in their classroom matters.

For months, I have been inundated by reports from teachers and teacher educators about how their professional lives are driven by expectations for raising students' test scores. These expectations come from no single, clearly defined source; they are simply part of a ubiquitous surround.

A colleague asked if I would take over a couple of sessions of his class. The students were in the first month of a graduate teacher education program and had just returned from a week in the schools. They had hoped to get a broad perspective on what being a schoolteacher is all about; instead, most felt cheated. Their concerns spilled forth: Was there any hope that this overriding preoccupation with tests might soon end?

Their frustrations were still on my mind when I settled down one evening with *The Art of the Commonplace,* by Wendell Berry. The book cautioned about the dangers of local matters of daily life coming under the control of distant "expert" bureaucracies, making them "world problems" requiring "world solutions," taking over from the people intimately familiar with the circumstances. This usurpation of local intelligence is colonizing many domains of modern life.

Berry gave me just the right message for my colleague's class. It has been a long time since I read Milton's *Paradise Lost,* but with this passage in hand, we had a great discussion of the moral credo that teachers must develop to maintain their own standards of teaching in a system plagued by outside experts.

—John I. Goodlad

College Professor
Washington

Paradise Lost, Book VIII

. . . apte the Mind or Fancie is to roave
Uncheckt, and of her roaving is no end;
Till warn'd, or by experience taught, she learn
That not to know at large of things remote
From use, obscure and suttle, but to know
That which before us lies in daily life,
Is the prime Wisdom, what is more, is fume,
Or emptiness, or fond impertinence,
And renders us in things that most concerne
Unpractis'd, unprepar'd, and still to seek.
Therefore from the high pitch let us descend
A lower flight, and speak of things at hand
Useful. . . .

—John Milton

I grew up with the American musical. I learned of the arts, music, and history from *Oklahoma, South Pacific,* and *My Fair Lady.* When I began teaching middle school, I used musicals to teach comprehension and character development. The way to Shakespeare was through *West Side Story,* and a discussion of prejudice and racism could begin with Rogers and Hammerstein's haunting "Carefully Taught" from *South Pacific.*

When I first saw *Into the Woods,* I was inspired by the teaching and learning at the story's core. The musical unites Cinderella, Little Red Ridinghood, and Jack (of the beanstalk) as they venture into the woods. Drawing on the philosophy of child psychologist Bruno Bettelheim, the woods is the place where inner darkness is confronted and where uncertainty is resolved about who one is and who one wants to be. The musical is a journey of growth and self-discovery.

Teaching is such a journey—a place where our fears are confronted daily and our uncertainty is constantly center stage. We are watched. We are listened to. Students can sense sincerity. They know when we care . . . when we're prepared . . . when they matter.

I listen to "Children Will Listen" at least four times a year. The words are on a bulletin board near my desk. They're a constant inspiration and celebration of the dignity that our students deserve and the dignity and responsibility of the wonderful profession of teaching.

—Don Shalvey
Superintendent
California

Children Will Listen

Careful the things you say,
Children will listen.
Careful the things you do,
Children will see.
And learn.
Children may not obey,
But children will listen.
Children will look to you
For which way to turn,
To learn what to be.
Careful before you say,
"Listen to me."
Children will listen.

Careful the wish you make,
Wishes are children.
Careful the path they take—
Wishes come true,
Not free.
Careful the spell you cast,
Not just on children.
Sometimes the spell may last
Past what you can see
And turn against you. . . .

Careful the tale you tell,
That is the spell.
Children will listen.

—*Stephen Sondheim*

I begin by reading this poem to a circle of twenty-five prospective teachers. As we let the powerful poem work on our imaginations, I ask, "What do you fear as you think about starting your career?" Tentatively, the twenty-two-year-old future social studies teacher responds, "I fear that I won't be able to motivate students and stimulate their desire to learn." A thirty-four-year-old mother of three shares her fear that classroom conduct will be uncontrollable. Others fear that their questions will be answered with blank stares, and that they will be told they can't teach the way they desire. The first honest responses set a tone and others rush to share their fear of student rejection, not knowing enough, becoming rigid, creating walls of isolation, and becoming bitter and burnt out.

Slowly this cathartic conversation allows them to move beyond their fears toward their hopes, values, and dreams. Whether the group consists of pre-service teachers, K–12 educators, or college professors, I have found that this poem provides a bridge to talking about the deeper aspects of our work. We begin to move beyond the "coward's silence," to take risks, so we can "keep the music playing." The powerful questions generated by this poem provide clues that allow us to create those magical moments in the classroom when we are connected to engaging ideas and to each other.

—Ron Petrich
College Professor
Minnesota

Love in the Classroom—*for my students*

Afternoon. Across the garden, in Green Hall,
someone begins playing the old piano—
a spontaneous piece, amateurish and alive,
full of a simple, joyful melody.
The music floats among us in the classroom.

I stand in front of my students
telling them about sentence fragments.
I ask them to find the ten fragments
in the twenty-one-sentence paragraph on
      page forty-five.
They've come from all parts
of the world—Iran, Micronesia, Africa,
Japan, China, even Los Angeles—and
      they're still
eager to please me. It's less than half
way through the quarter.

They bend over their books and begin.
Hamid's lips move as he follows
the tortuous labyrinth of English syntax.
Yoshie sits erect, perfect in her pale make-up,
legs crossed, quick pulse minutely
jerking her right foot. Tony,
from an island in the South Pacific, sprawls
limp and relaxed in his desk.

The melody floats around and through us
in the room, broken here and there,
      fragmented,

re-started. It feels Mideastern, but
it could be jazz, or the blues—it could be
anything from anywhere.
I sit down on my desk to wait,
and it hits me from nowhere—a sudden,
sweet, almost painful love for my students.

"Nevermind," I want to cry out.
"It doesn't matter about fragments.
Finding them or not. Everything's
a fragment and everything's not a fragment.
Listen to the music, how fragmented,
how whole, how we can't separate the music
from the sun falling on its knees on all the
      greenness,
from this moment, how this moment
contains all the fragments of yesterday
and everything we'll ever know of
      tomorrow!"

Instead, I keep a coward's silence.
The music stops abruptly;
they finish their work,
and we go through the right answers,
which is to say
we separate the fragments from the whole.

—Al Zolynas

Having spent a good deal of my career in the classroom teaching ten-year-olds, I find that Billy Collins's poem brings me right into that bittersweet territory of fence-sitting between childhood and adolescence. One moment there is innocence and light, the next, sadness and blood. The age is too delicious and too painful to remember accurately—a reason I am thankful for the poem. At first I thought this poem was about a boy, then I quickly remembered young girls who at four were "Arabian wizards" and at seven quite well-known soldiers and princes, thank you very much!

Early in the last century, Arnold Gesell, pioneering physician in the field of child development, wrote, "The best measure of the civilization of any people is the degree of thoughtful reverence paid to the child." Our civilization isn't measuring up. Our leaders talk glibly about leaving no child behind, when we in fact are in danger of leaving childhood behind in the wake of our own preoccupations.

When you teach children every day and go home to the evening news, you live very close to the wistfulness this poem evokes. What do I mean? Drive around your neighborhood. Where have all the children and their bicycles gone?

Now, I teach teachers and parents about ten-year-olds. I describe age ten as "the end of childhood." There is an audible gasp. It is the late afternoon light.

—Chip Wood
Elementary School Principal
Massachusetts

On Turning Ten

The whole idea of it makes me feel
like I'm coming down with something,
something worse than any stomach ache
or the headaches I get from reading in bad
    light—
a kind of measles of the spirit,
a mumps of the psyche,
a disfiguring chicken pox of the soul.

You tell me it is too early to be looking back,
but that is because you have forgotten
the perfect simplicity of being one
and the beautiful complexity introduced by
    two.
But I can lie on my bed and remember
    every digit.
At four I was an Arabian wizard.
I could make myself invisible
by drinking a glass of milk a certain way.
At seven I was a soldier, at nine a prince.

But now I am mostly at the window
watching the late afternoon light.
Back then it never fell so solemnly
against the side of my tree house,
and my bicycle never leaned against the
    garage
as it does today,
all the dark blue speed drained out of it.

This is the beginning of sadness, I say to
    myself,
as I walk through the universe in my
    sneakers.
It is time to say goodbye to my imaginary
    friends,
time to turn the first big number.

It seems only yesterday I used to believe
there was nothing under my skin but light.
If you cut me I would shine.
But now when I fall upon the sidewalks of
    life,
I skin my knees. I bleed.

—*Billy Collins*

When I began teaching, I started a "Feel Good" scrapbook. Inside are notes, cards, letters, student reflections, and awards—items that shield me from negativity and serve to lift my spirit. Occasionally, when I'm having one of those days where I have lost sight of the reasons I'm teaching, I pull this book out of my desk and read.

"The Gift" is the one poem in my scrapbook. I first encountered it in the summer of 1987, my first year as a teacher, and have been returning to it ever since.

Why do I find comfort in this poem? Because more than ever it is a difficult time to be a teacher. We are told we must effectively teach more standards in a school year than is humanly possible. The "No Child Left Behind" movement applies constant pressure to push students to perform on shallow, mandated standardized exams. Test preparation is forcing out real learning.

Amid these pressures, "The Gift" reminds me that it's my responsibility to teach students more than how to underline an adjective, identify a theme, or bubble in an answer sheet. There is a deeper curriculum. Much like the father in the poem who passes on compassion and tenderness to his son, I like to think that when I teach I will be sharing some of these gifts with my students. The same gifts I received from the fine teachers in my life.

—Kelly Gallagher
District English Curriculum Specialist
California

The Gift

To pull the metal splinter from my palm
my father recited a story in a low voice.
I watched his lovely face and not the blade.
Before the story ended, he'd removed
the iron sliver I thought I'd die from.

I can't remember the tale,
but hear his voice still, a well
of dark water, a prayer.
And I recall his hands,
two measures of tenderness
he laid against my face,
the flames of discipline
he raised above my head.

Had you entered that afternoon
you would have thought you saw a man
planting something in a boy's palm,
a silver tear, a tiny flame.
Had you followed that boy
you would have arrived here,
where I bend over my wife's right hand.

Look how I shave her thumbnail down
so carefully she feels no pain.
Watch as I lift the splinter out.
I was seven when my father
took my hand like this,
and I did not hold that shard
between my fingers and think,
Metal that will bury me,
christen it Little Assassin,
Ore Going Deep for My Heart.
And I did not lift up my wound and cry,
Death visited here!
I did what a child does
when he's given something to keep.
I kissed my father.

—*Li-Young Lee*

I became a widow when my children were eight and eleven. I returned to the class-room a week later to face my students, whose empathy for me bled out of their eyes. I knew I had to say something to keep us all from falling into one of those holes in the universe. I forced myself to look up, smiled, and said, "So what's it like being single in the '80s?"

The relief of our laughter showed me that it was my job to calm the fear of others—my children, my students, my colleagues. My grief was saved for soli-tary moments late at night when I was swept into a torrent of writing that no one saw—page after page of journal entries, poems, scribblings on yellow pads.

The irony is that my work is writing and healing. I help writers produce nar-ratives that make sense of traumatic experiences.

When I discovered "The Journey" I suddenly believed what I already knew: that my hard-won knowledge of trauma and grief, writing and love, was my voice. The split intrinsic to higher education, between emotion and cognition, professional and personal, does not include me or my children or many stu-dents and colleagues. As Lucille Clifton once said, "Every pair of eyes facing you has probably experienced something you could not endure." The poem reminds me that this is the journey we are all on, for in truth we have only one life we can save.

—*Marian Mesrobian MacCurdy*

College Professor
New York

The Journey

One day you finally knew
what you had to do, and began,
though the voices around you
kept shouting
their bad advice—
though the whole house
began to tremble
and you felt the old tug
at your ankles.
"Mend my life!"
each voice cried.
But you didn't stop.
You knew what you had to do,
though the wind pried
with its stiff fingers
at the very foundations—
though their melancholy
was terrible.
It was already late
enough, and a wild night,
and the road full of fallen
branches and stones.

But little by little,
as you left their voices behind,
the stars began to burn
through the sheets of clouds,
and there was a new voice,
which you slowly
recognized as your own,
that kept you company
as you strode deeper and deeper
into the world,
determined to do
the only thing you could do—
determined to save
the only life you could save.

—*Mary Oliver*

I recall how angry I became as I read this poem for the first time, as a high school student. As a high school teacher, I recall how one of my students grew outraged as he heard it for the first time: "It's not fair, it's absurd and . . . what are 'true lovers' anyway?"

It was then that I realized for the first time why the simple words *"[God] has less pity on schoolchildren"* are so powerful. Living in Israel during these unbearably sad times, these words are a direct channel through which the despair of entire generations comes out so loud and clear. Generations of people who love and hate, weighed down by constant wars.

Even today, I choose to open my teacher training courses at the university with this same poem, year after year. We seek for the *"coins of compassion that Mother handed down to us."* This poem is a source of power for me, raising doubts and questions, and at the same time lighting my way through life, education, work, carried on in the shadow of the stricken root metaphors *"crawling on all fours in the burning sand to reach the first-aid station covered with blood."*

This poem is like a sandwich in my lunch box—you eat it but then tomorrow the sandwich is still there. The power of the poem's simple lines continues to strike me, more than twenty-five years on.

—Shifra Schonmann

College Professor
Israel

God Has Pity on Kindergarten Children

God has pity on kindergarten children.
He has less pity on schoolchildren.
And on grownups he has no pity at all,
he leaves them alone,
and sometimes they must crawl on all fours
in the burning sand
to reach the first-aid station
covered with blood.

But perhaps he will watch over true lovers
and have mercy on them and shelter them
like a tree over the old man
sleeping on a public bench.

Perhaps we too will give them
the last rare coins of compassion
that Mother handed down to us,
so that their happiness will protect us
now and in other days.

—*Yehuda Amichai*

My career in education started with the kids no one else wanted to teach. I worked with adjudicated juvenile offenders in a wilderness-based treatment program affiliated with Pacific Crest Outward Bound School. My students already had been labeled *thief, robber, rapist,* and even *murderer,* most of them before they were sixteen years old. These were the kids many people had given up on; many of them were the kids who had given up on themselves.

In a way our work with these kids was simple; all we had to do was not become another adult who had given up on them, to show them they had things inside them that did not deserve to be abandoned. So we took these kids to the woods. Away from the influences, memories, and patterns that told them they were not worth anything. There we slowly and patiently peeled back the layers of pain and doubt to find that golden core worth believing in, the shy core that lurks in every person.

Rumi's poem reminded me that the lame and sick, those disfigured by the torture of their own deeds, still had wisdom and truth inside them. I often needed the reminder of "The Lame Goat" to keep my own discouragement from obscuring that truth. My work had (and still has) one basic premise for its foundation: Never give up on a kid—how can you help them to see their promise if you cannot see it yourself?

—*Michael Poutiatine*

High School Teacher
Washington

The Lame Goat

You've seen a herd of goats
going down to the water.

The lame and dreamy goat
brings up the rear.

There are worried faces about that one,
but now they're laughing,

because look, as they return,
that goat is leading!

There are many different kinds of knowing.
The lame goat's kind is a branch
that traces back to the roots of presence.

Learn from the lame goat,
and lead the herd home.

—*Jellaludin Rumi*

Listening to this poem stirred up childhood memories of when I too did not fit in, although for different reasons. I had pigtails, not a page boy; wore Aunt Hilda's old crepe dresses, not pleated plaid skirts and Peter Pan-collared blouses. My father, an immigrant, was strict, had a temper; I was afraid of him. I remembered how difficult it was to be separate, apart. I remembered the kindness of teachers.

When I share this poem with my students, they respond to its power, poignancy, and passion. They trust the honesty of the voice and readily enter into discussion, sharing their own experiences and those of others. One says she didn't know you could write about such things. Another, who lost a mother to death and a father to drugs, has been writing about it. They note how the personal connects with the universal, how violence transmutes to hopefulness because of compassion. When asked why the teacher took their excuses, they answer, because she'd been there and knew the importance of understanding.

This is a poem I need to read periodically to remind myself that students enter the classroom with emotional baggage—bricks packed beside texts inside school bags. In teaching the "whole child," I must remember that they are not "whole," but are, in fact, fractured. I need to be observant. The presence of this poem inspires and guides me to make of *myself* "each day a chink / a few might pass through unscathed."

—Wanda S. Praisner
Elementary School Teacher
New Jersey

Hotel Nights with My Mother

The hometown flophouse
was what she could afford
the nights he came after us
with a knife. I'd grab my books,
already dreading the next day's
explanations of homework undone
—*I ran out of paper*—the lies
I'd invent standing in front of
the nuns in the clothes I'd lain in
full-bladdered all night, a flimsy
chair-braced door between us
and the hallway's impersonal riot.

Years later, then, in the next
city, standing before my first class,
I scanned the rows of faces,
their cumulative skill in the
brilliant adolescent dances
of self-presentation, of hiding.
New teacher, looking young, seeming
gullible, I know, I let them
give me any excuse and took it.
I was watching them all

for the dark-circled eyes,
yesterday's crumpled costume, the marks
—the sorrowful coloring of marks—
the cuticles flaming and torn.
I made of myself each day a chink
a few might pass through unscathed.

—*Linda McCarriston*

My friend Lucile, a writer who teaches and teacher who writes, weaves both talents seamlessly into her life. Plainly speaking she's the best teacher I know. She listens to her students, seeing through teen facades to wholeness, heart, and possibility. Her classes, like yoga, stretch her students, building flexibility and strengthening backbone; and her students speak more clearly and honestly after a year with her. Lucile sent me "Melissa Quits School" in 1999. It still hangs on my wall, a reminder of the many students who are poorly served by high school and can't hold out until June.

Throughout my teaching career I've personally known too many Melissas. Sometimes they've chosen to tell me how dumb they feel, how angry they are at treatment received, at their assigned place in school. Often I've tried to convince them to stick it out—that things might get better. Ironically, for some, their leave-taking from school has been a resilient vote of belief in themselves.

Now I work to reinvent high school systems, and I reread "Melissa" often. Her story reminds me to see school through students' eyes, to keep their voices audible and their leadership present as we create schools that work for everyone.

I cringe at the thought that Melissa and others like her walk the halls at high school every day, feeling like losers and toughening themselves against the various assaults they perceive. Melissa reminds me that we've much work yet to do.

—Leslie Rennie-Hill

Foundation Director, High School Reform
Oregon

Melissa Quits School

I'm not going down into that cave anymore,
that room *under* everything
where they stick us freaks
surrounded by storage rooms
and one hundred years of dust
caking little windows near the ceiling.

We're buried under the weight
of all those rooms above us,
regular rooms with regular kids,
buried where we won't be a bad influence.

Mrs. Miller says I'll be sorry,
but I don't care. I can't think
down there. It's hard to breathe
underground.
If school's so great for my future,
what's Mrs. Miller doing buried here
like some sad dead bird
teaching freaks
and smelling like booze every morning?

I may be stupid, but I know this:
outside there'll be light and air
and I won't feel like I'm dying.
Outside, someone will pay when I work,
give me a coffee break when I can smoke.
No one will say "where's your pass?"
Sandy and Tina won't dance away from me,

sidestepping like I'm poison ivy,
and boys won't try to pry me open.
Steve won't be hanging on me,
wanting me
to take a couple of hits before class,
wanting me
to cut class to make love,
even though it's really screwing
and he calls it "making love"
so I'll do it and he can brag later.

I may be stupid, but I know this:
even just a little light and air
can save your life.
That shark Steve thinks he owns me,
but I know this:
when we cruise in his car
so he can show off his Chevy and me
him looking out the window all the time,
going nowhere, just cruising,
I'm there 'cause we're moving,
I'm there alone with Tori Amos,
singing her sad true songs,
leaning my head back,
watching the streetlights come and go,
each flash lighting my face
for a minute in the dark.

—*Lucile Burt*

Holding On

*T*eaching has many moments when the work feels too hard and we feel too weary—days when we walk out of class distraught by the apathy of our students or disenchanted by the lifeless priorities of the institution. We all experience stretches during a school year when time oozes by and the grind of each day takes its toll. We may even experience spans of time when we seriously question our decision to teach. Teaching is so public, so out in the open, there is little opportunity to hide.

In this section, teachers describe how they turn to poems to help them hold on to their heart and cling to those noble ideals that drew them to this work. These teachers salvage their hearts and revitalize their presence in the classroom by confronting that which drains their passion for this work. These teachers wrestle with their imperfections, take on their fears, reach out to colleagues, and seek out new ways to do their familiar tasks.

Inattention. Apathy. Fatigue. I confess to all of these and more at times in my role as teacher (and human being, for that matter). A friend once gave me a great definition of a calling: It's what calls you. While that is certainly what teaching does to me, sometimes I turn away, I forget or refuse to honor my calling. This poem reminds me of its presence and urges me to respond.

Sometimes it is the students themselves who, often unwittingly, reorient me. I remember Dwayne, whose sole purpose during my first year in teaching, I was sure, was to torment me. Any assignment I gave he met with groans of protest and attempts to inspire class mutiny. Then our principal, who had Dwayne in her daily advisory group, told me he'd announced with pride and some amazement that the novel we had read in class was the first book he had ever read cover to cover. Layers of frustration washed away from me and the mountain reappeared from the mist.

Levertov served as a civilian nurse in London during the bombings of World War II. I'm confident that if she could reconfirm that witnessing presence during her trials, I should be able to find my way as well. Whether it's my colleagues who extend guiding hands, or my students, or just an inexplicable clearing of my sight, the sense of purpose and calling that first brought me to teaching remains, witnessing and waiting for me to grab hold.

—Robert Kunzman
High School English Teacher and Administrator
Indiana

Witness

Sometimes the mountain
is hidden from me in veils
of cloud, sometimes
I am hidden from the mountain
in veils of inattention, apathy, fatigue,
when I forget or refuse to go
down to the shore or a few yards
up the road, on a clear day,
to reconfirm
that witnessing presence.

—*Denise Levertov*

The graduate students with whom I work are studying to become psychother-apists and organizational consultants. Theirs is no easy curriculum; it requires a commitment to learning and self-exploration, to honest communication and emotional integrity. And this is expected not only from the students but from faculty as well.

Some days my own commitment and resilience are truly tested. Some students I find difficult to reach and sometimes what happens in the classroom so mirrors the rage and pain in the world that I feel absolutely helpless and small. When these things occur, when people square off against one another in angry debate, when someone closes down in hurt or discloses a trauma too horrible to imagine, I return to Octavio Paz's poem "After." I find sustenance in the poem's idea that even after we abandon ourselves, lose all our hope, and push others away, there is still, within us and around us, the formidable persistence of "spirit."

Many of us in the West tend to be hard on ourselves; as adult learners we feel exposed by the learning process, sometimes humiliated and ashamed. Paz reminds us that it is our own doing: the judging and sentencing, the perpetual waiting and loneliness that such criticism inflicts. But even after we have for-gotten our names and the places of our birth, the heart still has the capacity to open again to love. Hearing this helps me weather the difficult moments in my work and my life.

—Catherine Johnson
College Professor
Washington

After

After chopping off all the arms that reached out to me;
after boarding up all the windows and doors;

after filling all the pits with poisoned water;
after building my house on the rock of a No
inaccessible to flattery and fear;

after cutting off my tongue and eating it;
after hurling handfuls of silence and monosyllables of scorn at my loves;

after forgetting my name
and the name of my birthplace
and the name of my race;

after judging and sentencing myself
to perpetual waiting
and perpetual loneliness, I heard
against the stones of my dungeon of syllogisms

the humid, tender, insistent
onset of spring.

—*Octavio Paz*

At the end of my second week of teaching, exhausted and discouraged, I reached for "Wild Geese," the poem that had caught me—held me—consoled me through college.

Once again, it grounded me, supplying the sort of perspective I associate with mountaintops after a wearying hike. I read it each morning before I set off for school, read it again at night whenever my anxieties and doubts about my capacity as a teacher (and my sanity for getting into this in the first place) loomed largest. I'm not entirely sure I would have stayed in teaching without it.

In late October of that first year, I put a copy of the poem on my office door, a quiet signal that I was ready to settle into the space, the profession, the life. I also intended it as an invitation to others it might touch, who might need the solace it offers, inviting them into my office, into a conversation with me and the poem.

The poem has been on my office door ever since, positioned so that anyone who enters the room must read it. It has become my credo about teaching (and living), a reminder of the central importance of hearing the stories of my students and telling my own, of the value of silence while staring into a swirling snowstorm and hearing its story. For me, this is a poem of solace and hope, imagination and rumination—why I became and remain a teacher.

—Elizabeth V. V. Bedell

High School English Teacher
Massachusetts

Wild Geese

You do not have to be good.
You do not have to walk on your knees
for a hundred miles through the desert, repenting.
You only have to let the soft animal of your body
    love what it loves.
Tell me about despair, yours, and I will tell you mine.
Meanwhile the world goes on.
Meanwhile the sun and the clear pebbles of the rain
are moving across the landscapes,
over the prairies and deep trees,
the mountains and the rivers.
Meanwhile the wild geese, high in the clean blue air,
are heading home again.
Whoever you are, no matter how lonely,
the world offers itself to your imagination,
calls to you like the wild geese, harsh and exciting—
over and over announcing your place
in the family of things.

—Mary Oliver

This verse feels right to me. It resonates, as a kind of music, with a feeling I often have about teaching. Teaching consumes me. At night I grind away my teeth over the previous day's events and the next day's possibilities. I come home from school ravenous for chocolate, for sugar, to restore my depleted blood substance. Weekends, summers, are barely long enough to restore an even tempo to my walking, my breathing.

And I wouldn't have it any other way.

Teaching feels like it means something. If Khalil (age thirteen) finally learns to read, that victory "flames upon the night." If a group of colleagues in our beleaguered public system feel that they choose to work at our school, that's another victory to flame upon the night. I love being alive with the heart-sap to feed these transient victories.

—*Betsy Wice*
Elementary School Teacher
Pennsylvania

Everything That Man Esteems

Everything that man esteems
Endures a moment or a day.
Love's pleasure drives his love away,
The painter's brush consumes his dreams;
The herald's cry, the soldier's tread
Exhaust his glory and his might:
Whatever flames upon the night
Man's own resinous heart has fed.

—*William Butler Yeats*

I remember the sense of near desperation I sometimes felt as a first-year high school teacher of 163 ninth- and tenth-grade literature students. Occasionally I escaped into my cubbyhole of an office during twenty-minute lunch breaks. I would turn off the lights and lie on my back on the cold, hard floor. I needed an escape because I was always running—personally invested in so many different students at once that I couldn't find myself in the chaos of all my feelings and good intentions. I continue to grapple with this tension—this drive to really "see" my students while realizing that I can see them only when I am spiritually still enough to acknowledge myself (to "feel my own weight and density").

When I first read May Sarton's poem, I was deeply struck with its relevance to my life—and it has become, in a sense, a personal credo. I am becoming more proactive in my search for the silent, poignant moment of self-recognition Sarton describes. If we do indeed teach who we are, then my search for authenticity may ultimately be as relevant to my students as it is to me.

I see life as a quest for the growing self-awareness portrayed in Sarton's poem, and my hope is that, through my teaching, my students and I will become more and more ourselves—attuned to the joyful and healing moment Sarton captures in her poem.

—Amy Eva-Wood

Instructor, Teacher Education Program
Washington

Now I Become Myself

Now I become myself. It's taken
Time, many years and places;
I have been dissolved and shaken,
Worn other people's faces,
Run madly, as if Time were there,
Terribly old, crying a warning,
"Hurry, you will be dead before—"
(What? Before you reach the morning?
Or the end of the poem is clear?
Or love safe in the walled city?)
Now to stand still, to be here,
Feel my own weight and density!
The black shadow on the paper
Is my hand; the shadow of a word
As thought shapes the shaper
Falls heavy on the page, is heard.
All fuses now, falls into place
From wish to action, word to silence,
My work, my love, my time, my face
Gathered into one intense
Gesture of growing like a plant.
As slowly as the ripening fruit
Fertile, detached, and always spent,
Falls but does not exhaust the root,
So all the poem is, can give,
Grows in me to become the song,
Made so and rooted so by love.

Now there is time and Time is young.
O, in this single hour I live
All of myself and do not move.
I, the pursued, who madly ran,
Stand still, stand still, and stop the sun!

—May Sarton

I was halfway into the passage before I realized that what I was reading was deeply personal, full of pain—and hope—shattering. I cried, in sadness for the utter pain in the words and then in joy for their inescapable truth and beauty. I resonated deeply to "the complex and inextricable caring for each other," finding comfort and courage in those words, while experiencing a growing fear at the realization that I wanted, no, needed, to "ride the monsters down" and that to do so would require first looking the monsters in the eye.

Annie Dillard's words sit on a page, a little crinkled and stiff with two faint coffee circles, under the lamp next to my bed. I read them often. Two years ago they inspired me to walk deep into the woods to find my selves, converse and make my peace with them, accepting that my crooked, cowering, fearful self had taught me courage and that my strength had its roots in my weak, self-doubting, even self-accusing, self.

The passage still echoes in my personal and professional life as I recover from a painful divorce and find new love, as I receive comfort and care in my battle with the loneliness and uncertainty of breast cancer, as I move from the accomplishments in thirty-five years of teaching young adults to the challenges of teaching teachers. In a broader sense the now-familiar words help me process recent world-shifting events, encouraging despair to partner with hope.

—Libby Roberts

High School Teacher Development Coordinator
Washington

From *Teaching a Stone to Talk*

In the deeps are the violence and terror of which psychology has warned us. But if you ride these monsters deeper down, if you drop with them farther over the world's rim, you find what our sciences cannot locate or name, the substrate, the ocean or matrix or ether which buoys the rest, which gives goodness its power for good, and evil its power for evil, the unified field: our complex and inexplicable caring for each other, and for our life together here. This is given. It is not learned.

—*Annie Dillard*

My friend sent me this poem today. I am not too tired to read a poem.

This year, as every year, I am overwhelmed by the amount of responsibilities I am given. I am too tired to stop and figure out what to do differently. I am discouraged with trying to live a balanced life.

I have been teaching elementary-age children for twenty years in both private and public schools. My transition to public schools was difficult. I missed the feeling of community based on a celebrated mission of teaching. My experience in Courage to Teach, a teacher renewal retreat program, provided me with the opportunity to feel connected with other teachers by going inward and trusting that they also would go inward and find meaning to share. Poetry became a member of our group. Our community formed around the four seasons, nature, silence, poetry, and our selves instead of around our common profession. It gently brought me to life in a public school setting. I was able to flow more and resist less.

And after reading this poem and going into "sweet darkness," I am reminded to try to do less by doing away with what doesn't bring the children and me alive.

—Jeanine O'Connell
Elementary School Teacher
Washington

Sweet Darkness

When your eyes are tired
the world is tired also.

When your vision has gone
no part of the world can find you.

Time to go into the dark
where the night has eyes
to recognize its own.

There you can be sure
you are not beyond love.

The dark will be your womb
tonight.

The night will give you a horizon
further than you can see.

You must learn one thing.
The world was made to be free in.

Give up all the other worlds
except the one to which you belong.

Sometimes it takes darkness and the sweet
confinement of your aloneness
to learn

anything or anyone
that does not bring you alive

is too small for you.

                              —*David Whyte*

I met this poem with the heaviest of hearts, a depleted spirit, a feeling that I was failing myself and my own personal mission. I was desperately in search of a renewal of hope, deeply in need of a reminder of what had led me into teaching in the first place. It seemed that no matter how hard we worked, those who benefitted most from educational reforms were the white students of privilege, while students of color and poor students fell further and further behind.

But Alves reminded me that "hope is the hunch that the overwhelming brutality of facts . . . is not the last word." Thus, with renewed understanding that the dates I plant may not be ones I ever have the opportunity to eat, and that the seeds of education and learning I plant within students may take years to grow, I recommitted myself to the work. I reclaimed my hope and belief in the notion that education could truly be the great equalizer. I convinced myself that the tremendous disparity in achievement between white students and students of color did not have to last forever, and that indeed, I could be an agent of change.

This poem is taped to my office wall to serve as a daily reminder that tomorrow's children deserve nothing less than a full and total commitment from me, and to continue to provide that, I must maintain hope—hope in those things seen and those unseen.

—Sarah Smith

Academic Director, Rainier Scholars
Washington

Tomorrow's Child

What is hope?
It is the pre-sentiment that imagination
is more real and reality is less real than it looks.
It is the hunch that the overwhelming brutality
of facts that oppress and repress us
is not the last word.
It is the suspicion that reality is more complex
than the realists want us to believe.
That the frontiers of the possible are not
determined by the limits of the actual;
and in a miraculous and unexplained way
life is opening up creative events
which will open the way to freedom and resurrection—
but the two—suffering and hope
must live from each other.
Suffering without hope produces resentment and despair.
But, hope without suffering creates illusions, naïveté
and drunkenness.
So let us plant dates
even though we who plant them will never eat them.
We must live by the love of what we will never see.
That is the secret discipline.
It is the refusal to let our creative act
be dissolved away by our need for immediate sense experience
and it a struggled commitment to the future of our grandchildren.
Such disciplined hope is what has given prophets, revolutionaries and saints,
the courage to die for the future they envisage.
They make their own bodies the seed of their highest hopes.

—Rubin Alves

As a teacher of young children, I love Donald Hall's picture book, *Ox Cart Man*, and eagerly share it with my students each fall. There is simple beauty in the way it presents work and the cycle of a year. Upon discovering "Names of Horses" I was primed for further lessons.

But how could this poem speak to me? This poem is about *horses!* Why does it touch me so? Perhaps it takes me back to a childhood love of farms. It certainly dignifies honest, effortful work and well-lived lives. And maybe sometimes in my teaching years I have felt like a workhorse. Long hours, repetitive tasks, the challenge of perseverance: maybe I see glimpses of myself in the staying power of those horses.

The poem reminds me of holiness even in the mundane. The detailed precision of Hall's language in describing the cycle of seasons within the cycle of tasks eloquently honors the act of labor. It reminds me of the pattern in all, that life moves along and even small things have their place, are significant beyond their moment.

And the poem's end: poignant in its letting go, tender in its remembering, life supported by the "soil makers" even after death. I love the way the poem suddenly, in its final line, makes the horses so personal, so individual. And I guess in the end, as a teacher, that is what I hope for: to continue to nourish life, to be remembered specifically, tenderly.

—*Laurel Leahy*
Kindergarten Teacher
Wisconsin

Names of Horses

All winter your brute shoulders strained against
　　collars, padding
and steerhide over the ash hames, to haul
sledges of cordwood for drying through spring
　　and summer,
for the Glenwood stove next winter, and for the
　　simmering range.

In April you pulled cartloads of manure to
　　spread on the fields,
dark manure of Holsteins, and knobs of your
　　own clustered with oats.
All summer you mowed the grass in the
　　meadow and hayfield, the mowing
　machine
clacketing beside you, while the sun walked
　　high in the morning;

and after noon's heat, you pulled a clawed rake
　　through the same acres,
gathering stacks, and dragged the wagon from
　　stack to stack,
and the built hayrack back, up hill to the chaffy
　　barn,
three loads of hay a day hanging wide from the
　　hayrack.

Sundays you trotted the two miles to church
　　with the light load
of a leather quartertop buggy, and grazed in the
　　sound of hymns.
Generation on generation, your neck rubbed
　　the window sill

of the stall, smoothing the wood as the sea
　　smooths glass.

When you were old and lame, when your
　　shoulders hurt bending to graze,
one October the man who fed you and kept
　　you, and harnessed you every
　morning,
led you through corn stubble to sandy ground
　　above Eagle Pond,
and dug a hole beside you where you stood
　　shuddering in your skin,

and lay the shotgun's muzzle in the boneless
　　hollow behind your ear,
and fired the slug into your brain, and felled
　　you into your grave,
shoveling sand to cover you, setting goldenrod
　　upright above you,
where by next summer a dent in the ground
　　made your monument.

For a hundred and fifty years, in the pasture of
　　dead horses,
roots of pine trees pushed through the pale
　　curves of your ribs,
yellow blossoms flourished above you in
　　autumn, and in winter
frost heaved your bones in the ground—old
　　toilers, soil makers:

O Roger, Mackerel, Riley, Ned, Nellie, Chester,
　　Lady Ghost.

　　　　　　　　　　　　　　—Donald Hall

Coming from Montana, I have learned the art of fire building. I have tried different types of wood, different sizes of kindling, different ways of laying the logs. I used to pile the wood on, to no avail. Hard as I tried to fan the flames into existence, they would only smolder. But now, after years of practice, most times I can build a fire to warm our home.

So it is with teaching. After five years my "fire" was burning brightly. I thrived on the energy that ignites in a classroom. But I was exhausted at the end of the day and overwhelmed by the never-ending list of things to do for my work, my home, my family. After much soul-searching, I realized I was piling on too many logs too tightly and the flame inside me was beginning to wane—even smolder at times. I was desperate for some "space."

Children need space as well. The constant piling on of facts and figures, the demands of time and energy can quickly douse the flame—the energy that children bring to the classroom.

I am learning, for myself and for my students, to choose consciously the logs I place on my own fire, and to pay special attention to the spaces that invite reflection and warmth. Given this space between the logs, my students and I often witness the special beauty that ignites and takes on a life of its own.

—*Maggie Anderson*
Middle and High School Science Teacher
Montana

Fire

What makes a fire burn
is space between the logs,
a breathing space.
Too much of a good thing,
too many logs
packed in too tight
can douse the flames
almost as surely
as a pail of water would.

So building fires
requires attention
to the spaces in between,
as much as to the wood.

When we are able to build
open spaces
in the same way
we have learned
to pile on the logs,
then we can come to see how
it is fuel, and absence of the fuel
together, that make fire possible.

We only need to lay a log
lightly from time to time.
A fire
grows
simply because the space is there,
with openings
in which the flame
that knows just how it wants to burn
can find its way.

—*Judy Brown*

One of my girlfriends performed this poem during a talent show when we were in high school, and I fell in love with its sounds. I admired her confidence and passion in reciting it and began to mimic her poise and repeat the words in my head that same night. Later, I met it again as a college student in an African American literature course. My husband, a journalist, fell in love with it before we met and together we have nurtured a respect for the power of Walker's words.

At first this poem took me back to a place where I was strong and in control and confident. Now it stands as a reminder of all that has gone before to make it possible for me to be who I am. I try to use it to help people recognize the beauty of their heritage and the stories that make up the fabric of their existence. On hard days this poem reminds me that I am the hope, the second generation mentioned in the poem. It tells me to keep fighting, keep reaching, and keep passing on whatever I have gained.

Walker captures with grace the anger and the hope that fight endlessly for the teacher's heart. We are complex creatures. We all have strengths and weaknesses, shadow and light. This poem encourages me in the dark hours of my perceived failures and spurs me on to the next battleground.

—Tracy Swinton Bailey
High School English Teacher
South Carolina

For My People

For my people everywhere singing their slave songs repeatedly: their dirges and their ditties and their blues and jubilees, praying their prayers nightly to an unknown god, bending their knees humbly to an unseen power;

For my people lending their strength to the years, to the gone years and the now years and the maybe years, washing ironing cooking scrubbing sewing mending hoeing plowing digging planting pruning patching dragging along never gaining never reaping never knowing and never understanding;

For my playmates in the clay and dust and sand of Alabama backyards playing baptizing and preaching and doctor and jail and soldier and school and mama and cooking and playhouse and concert and store and hair and Miss Choomby and company;

For the cramped bewildered years we went to school to learn to know the reasons why and the answers to and the people who and the places where and days when, in memory of the bitter hours when we discovered we were black and poor and small and different and nobody cared and nobody wondered and nobody understood;

For the boys and girls who grew in spite of these things to be man and woman, to laugh and dance and sing and play and drink their wine and religion and success, to marry their playmates and bear children and then die of consumption and anemia and lynching;

For my people thronging 47th Street in Chicago and Lenox Avenue in New York and Rampart Street in New Orleans, lost disinherited dispossessed and happy people filling the cabarets and taverns and other people's pockets needing bread and shoes and milk and land and money and something—something all our own;

For my people walking blindly spreading joy, losing time being lazy, sleeping when
hungry, shouting when burdened, drinking when hopeless, tied and shackled and
tangled among ourselves by the unseen creatures who tower over us omnisciently and
laugh;

For my people blundering and groping and floundering in the dark of churches and
schools and clubs and societies, associations and councils and committees and
conventions, distressed and disturbed and deceived and devoured by money-hungry
glory-craving leeches, preyed on by facile force of state and fad and novelty, by false
prophet and holy believer;

For my people standing staring trying to fashion a better way from confusion, from
hypocrisy and misunderstanding, trying to fashion a world that will hold all the
people, all the faces, all the adams and eves and their countless generations;

Let a new earth rise. Let another world be born. Let a bloody peace be written in the sky.
Let a second generation full of courage issue forth; let a people loving freedom come
to growth. Let a beauty full of healing and a strength of final clenching be the pulsing
in our spirits and our blood. Let the martial songs be written, let the dirges disappear.
Let a race of men now rise and take control.

—*Margaret Walker*

In the Moment

*T*ouching, tasting, smelling, and hearing the particulars of life all pose a challenge for teachers, who often must work to a jarring rhythm and a feverish pace. The demands on teachers are frequently overwhelming. They have students to teach, lessons to plan, papers to grade, parents to contact, colleagues to meet, and committees to serve. Teachers often feel that their work is never done and that the needs of their students are never fulfilled.

But every classroom is a storehouse of miracles. If we keep our eyes peeled and listen with care, we can apprehend moments of mystery, beauty, and wonder. These are the moments in which we feel most alive. They are always there, waiting to be caught and savored, but without attention and presence they slip past. The poems in this section focus on learning to honor our limits, make peace with our imperfections, and create opportunities to be present with our students and colleagues in the moment.

This poem, written by a friend who died relatively young, immediately enchant-ed me. I hear her voice when I read it, and that's a gift in itself.

As I get older, I'm beginning to accept my imperfections with more grace. I've often come to love the learning from them. Sometimes I've sincerely wel-comed them into my life. But when I first read this poem, I realized how far I was from being in love with the imperfections themselves. And how I longed for that.

Rereading this poem helps me in my quest to honor the imperfections that are a daily part of teaching and life. After a tough day, I invite myself to love the many parts that were less than perfect. On the rare occasions when I've experi-enced that love at a deep level, I've glimpsed the freedom and self-acceptance so vivid in this poem. In those moments, I know that "learning to purr" is a grand goal, "the empty mind" a glorious pursuit (purr-suit?).

My relationship with this poem has been enriched by sharing it. When ask-ing learners to try something new or risky, I often start by reading it. As I speak, I hear rueful laughter and a collective sigh. Many listeners tell me that the poem freed them to risk and explore, to let go of the outcome. Their strong response reminds me anew that I am not alone in this quest, that many of us yearn to make deep and lasting friends with imperfection.

—*Glynis Wilson Boultbee*

Educational Consultant
Alberta, Canada

Imperfection

I am falling in love
    with my imperfections
The way I never get the sink really clean,
forget to check my oil,
lose my car in parking lots,
miss appointments I have written down,
am just a little late.

I am learning to love
    the small bumps on my face
    the big bump of my nose,
    my hairless scalp,
chipped nail polish,
toes that overlap.
Learning to love
    the open-ended mystery
      of not knowing why

I am learning to fail
    to make lists,
    use my time wisely,
    read the books I should.

Instead I practice inconsistency,
    irrationality, forgetfulness.

Probably I should
hang my clothes neatly in the closet
all the shirts together, then the pants,
send Christmas cards, or better yet
a letter telling of
    my perfect family

But I'd rather waste time
listening to the rain,
or lying underneath my cat
    learning to purr.

I used to fill every moment
    with something I could
      cross off later.

Perfect was
    the laundry done and folded
    all my papers graded
    the whole truth and nothing   but

Now the empty mind is what I seek
    the formless shape
    the strange   off center
    sometimes fictional
        me.

—*Elizabeth Carlson*

"What do I do when I get lost in the forest?" This poem, based on the initiation quests of native peoples of the Northwest coast, attempts to answer this question. It speaks to me about the importance of slowing down and paying attention, and entering a place with a spirit of receptivity to what it might teach.

Going deeper, it speaks of how any experience of being lost can be an opportunity to let ourselves be found, by opening to the place where we are. This has sustained me as a teacher over the years: helping me to hang in there when I felt lost in a particular situation, or when I have lost the larger vision of my teaching. Pay attention to the place where you are, the poem reassures me: even a place of lostness can speak to you.

I often share the poem when I take a class on an outdoor walk. I recite the poem and suggest that everyone go off on their own to observe their surroundings and give the images of the poem a chance to speak. I invite them to notice the unique details of the place, how each tree or branch might be different to Raven or Wren; to reflect on how it feels to approach this place as a powerful stranger, and what it might have to teach them; and to reflect on what it might say to them about being lost, paying attention, and letting themselves be found.

—Fred Taylor
Adult Educator
Vermont

Lost

Stand Still. The trees ahead and bushes beside you
Are not lost. Wherever you are is called Here,
And you must treat it as a powerful stranger,
Must ask permission to know it and be known.
The forest breathes. Listen. It answers,
I have made this place around you.
If you leave it, you may come back again, saying Here.
No two trees are the same to Raven.
No two branches are the same to Wren.
If what a tree or a bush does is lost on you,
You are surely lost. Stand still. The forest knows
Where you are. You must let it find you.

—*David Wagoner*

I am a connector by nature. I love to draw lines between the dots of ideas, people, projects, opportunities. Most of the time it's a helpful trait. But sometimes I find myself "whelmed-over" by so many connections that my internal life becomes gridlocked. How do I find rest from the traffic jam of it all?

Just imagine. Every year, digging a hole in the ground and pouring in a year's worth of papers, e-mail, awards, mistakes, reports, assorted things I do not need any more. Sweep the desk clear. Empty the backpack. Compost it all!

Then add the waste accumulated within myself, "stuff" that bogs me down as I haul it around. Disappointments, and worse: doubts, resentments, remorse. Better to place them in the earth, giving thanks for whatever I've been able to learn. Better to make room for new growth in my soul.

How much my life can be improved by seeing that indeed I have not been grateful enough, all things considered. Realizing I have been "inattentive to wonders" that, despite the evening news, surround me each and every day: the sky, the wind, and the faithful "trees" of my many friends and family members. Let praise be sung to them!

Let me, by this ritual, honor the aliveness I wish to bring to my colleagues, my community, my family, and our world. Let my faith be in the deathless earth, from which all that is good arises, and to which all that lives returns.

—*Rick Jackson*

Co-Director, Center for Courage & Renewal
Washington

A Purification

At the start of spring I open a trench
in the ground. I put into it
the winter's accumulation of paper,
pages I do not want to read
again, useless words, fragments,
errors. And I put into it
the contents of the outhouse:
light of the sun, growth of the ground,
finished with one of their journeys.
To the sky, to the wind, then,
and to the faithful trees, I confess
my sins: that I have not been happy
enough, considering my good luck;
have listened to too much noise;
have been inattentive to wonders;
have lusted after praise.
And then upon the gathered refuse
of mind and body, I close the trench,
folding shut again the dark,
the deathless earth. Beneath that seal
the old escapes into the new.

                    —*Wendell Berry*

We humans put so much emphasis on *fast* in our world—we want everything from cheeseburgers to information instantly. Nature knows better. "Connections are made slowly." Piercy's words remind me of the importance of "the way things grow in the real world, slowly enough." That's how I want to grow—slowly enough.

I have taught this poem to many teachers. As we read the poem, faces of children pop up between the lines, reminding us that despite the manic pace of the world, children grow slowly enough if allowed. We feel affirmed by the line "You cannot always tell by looking what is happening" because we know how often learning takes place in ways we cannot see—and that tests cannot measure.

Teachers read Piercy's words aloud with wonder, often with reverence, sounding as if they are tasting them, savoring them. I know they are remembering that they, as well as their children, grow at their own rates—slowly enough. I know—because I do too.

—Sally Z. Hare
Teacher Educator
South Carolina

The seven of pentacles

Under a sky the color of pea soup
she is looking at her work growing away there
actively, thickly like grapevines or pole beans
as things grow in the real world, slowly enough.
If you tend them properly, if you mulch, if you water,
if you provide birds that eat insects a home and winter food,
if the sun shines and you pick off caterpillars,
if the praying mantis comes and the ladybugs and the bees,
then the plants flourish, but at their own internal clock.

Connections are made slowly, sometimes they grow underground.
You cannot tell always by looking what is happening.
More than half a tree is spread out in the soil under your feet.
Penetrate quietly as the earthworm that blows no trumpet.
Fight persistently as the creeper that brings down the tree.
Spread like the squash plant that overruns the garden.
Gnaw in the dark and use the sun to make sugar.

Weave real connections, create real nodes, build real houses.
Live a life you can endure: make love that is loving.
Keep tangling and interweaving and taking more in,
a thicket and bramble wilderness to the outside but to us
interconnected with rabbit runs and burrows and lairs.

Live as if you liked yourself, and it may happen:
reach out, keep reaching out, keep bringing in.
This is how we are going to live for a long time: not always,
for every gardener knows that after the digging, after
    the planting,
after the long season of tending and growth, the harvest comes.

—*Marge Piercy*

I have had a love affair with words ever since I cracked the code and read "Cinderella" on my own. This passion led me to spend my time encouraging eighth graders to discover the power of words, especially their own.

After 9/11, I tried to give my students opportunities to speak and write about the world and themselves. When a friend sent me Neruda's poem, I realized that what we needed was not more words but to stop for a while. We needed no more information; we were swimming in it. Together we read the poem, then sat in the quiet listening to our own hearts.

Neruda's quiet is not the silence of isolation but the quiet that connects us in community. Being quiet together is a profound acknowledgment of the interior life of each of us. It provides space to breathe, to remember, to question, to feel compassion, to connect to each other and ourselves. This quiet is not the absence of life but what sustains it.

My students are typical American teenagers who spend their days running from class to class, to athletics, to music lessons, to youth groups, with a few minutes in between for TV, radio, and CDs. When "the world is too much with us" with all its arm-waving and words that do not add but drain meaning from our experience, I pull out Neruda's poem and together we stop and savor "a delicious moment."

—*Catherine Gerber*
Middle School Teacher
Washington

Keeping Quiet

Now we will count to twelve
and we will all keep still.

This one time upon the earth,
let's not speak any language,
let's stop for one second,
and not move our arms so much.

It would be a delicious moment,
without hurry, without locomotives,
all of us would be together
in a sudden uneasiness.

The fishermen in the cold sea
would do no harm to the whales
and the peasant gathering salt
would look at his torn hands.

Those who prepare green wars,
wars of gas, wars of fire,
victories without survivors,
would put on clean clothing
and would walk alongside their brothers
in the shade, without doing a thing.

What I want shouldn't be confused
with final inactivity:
life alone is what matters,
I want nothing to do with death.

If we weren't unanimous
about keeping our lives so much in motion,
if we could do nothing for once,
perhaps a great silence would
interrupt this sadness,
this never understanding ourselves
and of threatening ourselves with death,
perhaps the earth is teaching us
when everything seems to be dead
and then everything is alive.

Now I will count to twelve
and you keep quiet and I'll go.

—*Pablo Neruda*

It's a powerful reminder that my pen and paper are tools, as is every detail in my life that I may use to my advantage. The first spring hyacinth just picked, its smell taking me back to my childhood where poems grow, gives me not only permission to schedule my own flights of fancy, but the necessity of thinking my "dry crusty thoughts," and all the other kinds, if I am ever to get anything right and "pass it on."

I discovered Snyder's poem and thumbtacked it above my desk where I could read it every time I looked up. It keeps me going when I become discouraged in my teaching or writing, because I fear I don't know enough.

I like to use this poem to inspire students to write about small, ordinary things from their world, things that become extraordinary by their simple attention. "Think of the beach where we live." I point out how each time we walk there, it is exquisitely different in how the light falls, the kinds of sea birds, the number of rocks and shells and the height of the waves.

Each day is also like that, and every student. Those "hard pleasant tasks" of preparing lessons, writing encouraging remarks, and meeting schedules can also uplift and nourish the soul, if we look between the spaces and beyond.

—Perie Longo

Teacher, Poets in the Schools Program
California

What Have I Learned

What have I learned but
the proper use for several tools?

The moments
between hard pleasant tasks

To sit silent, drink wine,
and think my own kind
of dry crusty thoughts.

—the first Calochortus flowers
    and in all the land,
        it's spring.
    I point them out:
    the yellow petals, the golden hairs,
        to Gen.

Seeing in silence:
never the same twice,
but when you get it right,
    you pass it on.

—*Gary Snyder*

My ninth- and tenth-grade classes spent the entire day watching television coverage of the attacks, journaling, and softly talking. The school was full of sorrow and disbelief. I felt frantic about one of my best friends, who taught near the World Trade Center and would have been starting work at about the time the planes struck. I shared my worries with the students. I could not hold back the tears.

Like every teacher in this country, I struggled with how and what to teach the following day. My answer was to dig up this poem, which was given to me by my students when I left after a year of teaching English in Poland.

Along with the poem, I brought in copies of a newspaper photo of a young man wearing a baseball cap, about my students' age, with his head in his arms on a ticket counter. He had arrived at JFK airport to discover that he had missed one of the highjacked planes by minutes. I used the poem and the photo to talk about the attack, my students' feelings for those who had died, their own and their loved ones' vulnerability, and my friend's narrow escape from death.

Since 9/11, I think of this poem often. I think of the original context of the poem, the Nazi occupation of Poland in World War II and the Holocaust. I think of the arbitrariness and unpredictability of life and how precious the present moment is.

—*Lesley Woodward*
High School English Teacher
Massachusetts

There But for the Grace

It could have happened.
It had to happen.
It happened sooner. Later.
Nearer. Farther.
It happened not to you.

You survived because you were the first.
You survived because you were the last.
Because you were alone. Because of people.
Because you turned left. Because you turned right.
Because rain fell. Because a shadow fell.
Because sunny weather prevailed.

Luckily there was a wood.
Luckily there were no trees.
Luckily there was a rail, a hook, a beam, a brake,
a frame, a bend, a millimeter, a second.
Luckily a straw was floating on the surface.

Thanks to, because, and yet, in spite of.
What would have happened had not a hand, a foot,
by a step, a hairsbreadth
by sheer coincidence.

So, you're here? Straight from a moment still ajar?
The net had one eyehole, and you got through it?
There's no end to my wonder, my silence.
Listen
how fast your heart beats in me.

—*Wislawa Szymborska*

As I approach my seventieth year, this poem speaks to me. Hopefully, my time of being the continual pleaser is past. Thankfully, the time of being caught up, constantly, in the personal agendas of others is past.

As a teacher and school principal who has joyfully given of my time and talent to others for almost fifty years, I now find myself—noticing myself. It's kind of a surprise. It's sort of a shock. I read the words of this poem gratefully, and I find the invitation given here to be reassuring and comforting.

As I greet myself anew, I find that I really like myself. I am pleased with my peaceful demeanor. I like the quiet steadiness. I love my almost feverish desire to create, to build. I am amazed by my newfound obligation to speak the truth. Feasting on my life makes my heart sing.

—David Hagstrom

Retired Principal
Alaska

Love After Love

The time will come
when, with elation,
you will greet yourself arriving
at your own door, in your own mirror,
and each will smile at the other's welcome,

and say, sit here. Eat.
You will love again the stranger who was your self.
Give wine. Give bread. Give back your heart
to itself, to the stranger who has loved you

all your life, whom you ignored
for another, who knows you by heart.
Take down the love letters from the bookshelf,

the photographs, the desperate notes,
peel your own image from the mirror.
Sit. Feast on your life.

—*Derek Walcott*

The present is elusive for those of us who teach. We are ever planning the next day's, week's, semester's lessons, ever planning the next weekend, new project, vacation, retirement. This poem calls me back to the present moment. It reminds me to pay attention to my physical surroundings, to the thoughts I'm thinking in that very moment, to the feelings that arise and move away, to my own breath. It is a practice I am trying to learn in yoga and meditation classes and in all of my life.

In my classroom, I have begun the practice of starting each class with silence. In the noise and busy-ness of the school day, I tell my students, we need time to stop and call our attention home in order to be ready for our work together. I began this practice of silence with trepidation, in fear of adolescent ridicule, but buoyed by Stafford's idea: "This interval you spent . . . keep it for life." I knew I needed something for lift, to carry me out of the feeling of racing from one class to the next. The silent time allowed me to start "here, right in this room." Surprisingly, after initial discomfort, the students report the same feeling of calm readiness for the work at hand. We are all reminded, "What can anyone give you greater than now?"

—Lucile Burt

High School English Teacher
Massachusetts

You Reading This, Be Ready

Starting here, what do you want to remember?
How sunlight creeps along a shining floor?
What scent of old wood hovers, what softened
sound from outside fills the air?

Will you ever bring a better gift for the world
than the breathing respect that you carry
wherever you go right now? Are you waiting
for time to show you some better thoughts?

When you turn around, starting here, lift this
new glimpse that you found; carry into evening
all that you want from this day. This interval you spent
reading or hearing this, keep it for life—

What can anyone give you greater than now,
starting here, right in this room, when you turn around?

—*William Stafford*

Life is filled with challenges, disappointments, and cares. "Don't Quit" tells me that the greatest opportunities come during these times; they are periods of growth and possibility, a sign that greater things are ahead. It's obvious that Edgar Guest faced many days when nothing seemed to go right. He says these are the days we should take a break, but never give up.

This poem hangs on my office wall, directly in front of my desk. When I feel tired, weary, and overwhelmed, I look up from my work and begin to read the words aloud. It's almost as if I hear Guest telling me, "don't quit," never give up. It gives me strength, hope, and revived energy to go on. I see the same hope in the eyes of educators who have faced tough challenges and unkind criticisms whenever I recite this poem at the end of a meeting. By the time I finish the first paragraph, I see their expressions change and new life on their faces.

"Don't Quit" reminds me that when I feel furthest from my goal, I am closer than I think. It's like coming out of a dark room into a well-lit hallway. So in this life filled with uncertainties, you must "stick to the fight, when you are hardest hit." And know that when you feel your worst, it's a signal that you can't stop; you must keep going and claim the victory that lies ahead.

—Reg Weaver

President, National Education Association
Washington, D.C.

Don't Quit

When things go wrong, as they sometimes will
When the road you are trudging seems all uphill,
When the funds are low and the debts are high,
And you want to smile but you have to sigh,
When care is pressing you down a bit,
Rest, if you must—but don't you quit!
Life is queer with its twists and turns,
As every one of us sometimes learns,
And many a failure turns about,
When he might have won had he stuck it out;
Don't give up, though the pace seems slow,
You might succeed with another blow.
Success is failure turned inside out
the silver tint of the clouds of doubt
And you can never tell how close you are,
It might be near when it seems afar;
So stick to the fight when you are hardest hit
It's when things get worse that you mustn't quit!

—*Edgar A. Guest*

Making Contact

o do our best teaching, we must stay connected. Connected to our inner life, our colleagues, our students, and the subjects we teach. When we work and live in isolation, we miss out on what we need most: empathy, shared wisdom, and communal expertise.

The teachers in this section share poems that allow them to keep heart and grow. Their message is that they are most alive and creative when they stay connected to their own dreams and aspirations while reaching out to companions who challenge them to continue learning about what it means to be a better teacher. These teachers resist those institutional and cultural forces that would cut them off from each other and their students. They listen deeply to themselves, each other, and their students, and in doing so create communities where learners and teachers can flourish.

A subject is most rich, surprising, exciting, fertile when we see beneath the surface. It is especially so for writing, the subject I teach. I believe a well-lived life is about this too—the courage to get at what's under the surface.

My exploration starts with a recognition that my whole life matters and that what matters is worth my time. It is a journey that shows me more about myself—and about teaching and learning—than any theory or formal education.

I share with students where my deeper roots come from, what the dirt is. In my childhood and teenage years I had many operations on my right leg because of a birth defect. At eighteen, my leg was amputated. I describe, with some care, how I was compelled to write to get through this painful experience—and through writing discovered an intense desire to express the fierce truth and a passion for beauty.

This exploration of my life, with its troubles, blessings, and challenges, takes courage. "These Days" gives me permission and inspiration to express my roots, to live and examine my life.

I've come to feel that the quality of presence, attention, sense of adventure, and inquiry I bring to a classroom results from leaving my roots on. This twenty-three-word poem, companion of many years, reminds me that a world of wholeness lives and will thrive within me when I "leave the roots on." That's the world of depth I strive to share.

—John Fox
College Professor
California

These Days

whatever you have to say, leave
the roots on, let them
dangle

And the dirt

    Just to make clear
    where they come from

        —Charles Olson

I never expected my dear friend Sally to put me in a place of emotional pain—yet she did. She read "The Bridge." My eyes filled with tears, my throat contracted, and my heart beat rapidly.

The poem stirred an inner (and carefully hidden) anger—rage toward the institutions and people who had forced me, in the name of being OK, to become a bridge over the troubled waters of racism, sexism, and insanity. I was not ready to say, "I am sick of being the bridge to this and that place for others," but goodness gracious me, the poet so eloquently said it for me. Permitting myself to feel and release the pain of being a bridge for everyone and their mother was soulfully exhilarating. No longer would I be held as an emotional hostage.

Although I was in pain, I could sense a freedom through the liberating words, "I must be the bridge to nowhere but my true self and then I will be useful." I relished the words *"I've had enough"* in my soul and the pain of freedom this new insight provided.

The poem continues its gracious impact on my personal and professional life. I am intentional in connecting to those who travel in life with me as mother, daughter, wife, teacher, minister, colleague, friend. To maintain joyful living, I retain in my soul's liberated membranes the poetic truth on which I stand: *The bridge I must be is the bridge to my own power.*

—*Debbie S. Dewitt*

Kindergarten Teacher
South Carolina

The Bridge Poem

I've had enough
I'm sick of seeing and touching
Both sides of things
Sick of being the damn bridge for everybody

Nobody can talk to anybody without me   Right

I explain my mother to my father my father to
my little sister my little sister to my brother my
brother to the White Feminists the White
Feminists to the Black Church Folks the Black
Church Folks to the ex-Hippies the ex-Hippies
to the Black Separatists the Black Separatists to
the Artists the Artists to the parents of my
friends . . .

Then
I've got to explain myself
To everybody

I do more translating than the U.N.

Forget it
I'm sick of filling in your gaps
Sick of being your insurance against
The isolation of your self-imposed limitations
Sick of being the crazy at your Holiday Dinners
The odd one at your Sunday Brunches
I am sick of being the sole Black friend to
Thirty-four Individual White Folks

Find another connection to the rest of the world
Something else to make you legitimate
Some other way to be political and hip
I will not be the bridge to your womanhood
Your manhood
Your human-ness

I'm sick of reminding you not to
Close off too tight for too long

Sick of mediating with your worst self
On behalf of your better selves

Sick
Of having
To remind you
To breathe
Before you
Suffocate
Your own
Fool self

Forget it
Stretch or drown
Evolve or die

You see   it's like this
The bridge I must be
Is the bridge to my own power
I must translate
My own fears
Mediate
My own weaknesses

I must be the bridge to nowhere
But my own true self
It's only then
I can be
Useful

—*Donna Kate Rushin*

Fridays during lunch my classroom fills with kids seeking a place they can call home. Many of these kids, to borrow from Heaney's poem, have suffered, been hurt, turned hard. Heaney writes, "No poem or play or song / Can fully right a wrong," but the kids who come to Word Up! would disagree.

These teenagers celebrate themselves, raising their voices in song and verse against the wrongs they've endured. They heal themselves and each other through the water of their words, finding the hope to "believe that a further shore is reachable from here."

I am not the one who heads this gathering. It is a quiet girl named Allison Molina, a junior who said that kids need a place to "say what they gotta say." When I hear Allison call for "respect!" as she convenes the Word Up! with a poem, I think of Heaney's lines:

> Call miracle self-healing,
> The utter self-revealing
> Double-take of feeling.

Heaney's poem is about Philocotetes, an injured soldier whom Odysseus abandoned. The kids that come on Fridays often seem to feel left behind, to have endured some injury. Heaney's words "outcry and the birth-cry / Of new life at its term" capture their efforts to give birth to themselves. Through words, through poetry, they cure themselves for that one hour when their hopes and hearts rhyme, while I sit in the back, bearing witness to their voices, their lives, and all they have to say if we can only find the courage to listen.

—Jim Burke
High School English Teacher
California

From "The Cure at Troy"

Human beings suffer.
They torture one another.
They get hurt and get hard.
No poem or play or song
Can fully right a wrong
Inflicted and endured.

History says, *Don't hope*
On this side of the grave,
But then, once in a lifetime
The longed-for tidal wave
Of justice can rise up
And hope and history rhyme.

So hope for a great sea-change
On the far side of revenge.
Believe that a farther shore
Is reachable from here.
Believe in miracles
And cures and healing wells.

Call miracle self-healing,
The utter self-revealing
Double-take of feeling.
If there's fire on the mountain
Or lightning and storm
And a god speaks from the sky

That means someone is hearing
The outcry and the birth-cry
Of new life at its term.
It means once in a lifetime
That justice can rise up
And hope and history rhyme.

—*Seamus Heaney*

When high school is all said and done, it comes down to the relationships students have built over the last four years. The cool part of this poem—which I read when I was studying to be a psychologist and have used at graduations since—is that if you think about it from the voice of a teacher, the greatest gift is not just that the students hear, understand, and touch *you,* but that you do the same for them. We must have respect for our students and see how strong relationships are at the center of any good school.

The joke of schools is that we assume that kids are walking in ready to learn, ready to have content poured into them. I would love it if that were true. But there is way more going on in a kid's mind than just school. You have got to teach the heart as well as the mind, and for that you have to make sure that the heart and mind are OK before you can even begin. So much is threatening our students' lives out there that we have got to make it safe "in here." It is nearly impossible to teach a kid who isn't ready to learn. It is absolutely impossible to teach a kid who is no longer here at all.

—Dennis Littky
High School Principal
Rhode Island

Making Contact

I believe
The greatest gift
I can conceive of having
from anyone
is
to be seen by them,
heard by them,
to be understood
and
touched by them.
The greatest gift
I can give
is
to see, hear, understand
and to touch
another person.
When this is done
I feel
contact has been made.

—*Virginia Satir*

Moffitt's provocative directive, "You must be the thing you see," challenges us to imagine life from other perspectives. Who am I? Who are we in relation to each other? With every reading, I am reminded to try to "know that thing," at least momentarily.

To be the student in that desk, struggling to read the text. To be the parent working two minimum-wage jobs, summoning courage to attend parent conference night. To be the colleague aching from a divorce or a death in the family, trying to wear a brave face each day while standing in front of students. To be the principal who in the name of accountability insults teachers' professionalism while secretly mourning the loss of his own zeal for teaching.

I am reminded to see my students as people with their own stories and to create ways for them to also "know the thing"—to help them connect with the assignments, with each other, and with me as a human being. To see me not only as a teacher of English but also as an adult embodiment of compassion— perhaps a person they would consider emulating one day. In class, we share with each other, revealing the readers and writers that we are. This allows us to "know the thing," with the *thing* being alternatively each other, a greater level of literacy, and a growing sense of empathy—"the very peace" we issue from.

—Angela Peery
High School English Teacher
South Carolina

To Look at Any Thing

To look at any thing,
If you would know that thing,
You must look at it long:
To look at this green and say,
'I have seen spring in these
Woods,' will not do—you must
Be the thing you see:
You must be the dark snakes of
Stems and ferny plumes of leaves,
You must enter in
To the small silences between
The leaves,
You must take your time
And touch the very peace
They issue from.

—*John Moffitt*

When the familiar palm-sweats started, I would turn within and ask simply, "What is the truth here?" The slowing down and going within helped me find words to tell my truth calmly and try to communicate it in a manner both illuminating and inoffensive to the other. This practice has helped me maintain balance and a sense of peace when tempted to bow to the pressures of the school culture.

I've been teaching for more than four decades, and never have I witnessed such a fascination with measuring and testing a sadly narrow form of intelligence. This challenges my values and beliefs, my vision of teaching and learning, and my manner of relating to students and colleagues. At these moments I turn to Rumi.

Any poem that is important to me I always share with my students. This one played a major role in my eighth graders' discussion of what counts as effective learning. In that discussion, Julie said, "Like Rumi talked about, what's most effective for me is when there is room for my inner voice. So much of our time is just spent repeating what the book says, or what the teacher says. It's not very often we get to actually say what we think. I think I really learn when I can share my own thoughts."

To teacher and student alike, Rumi keeps on giving.

—*Marianne Houston*
Retired Middle School Teacher
Michigan

Two Kinds of Intelligence

There are two kinds of intelligence: one acquired,
as a child in school memorizes facts and concepts
from books and from what the teacher says,
collecting information from the traditional sciences
as well as from the new sciences.

With such intelligence you rise in the world.
You get ranked ahead or behind others
in regard to your competence in retaining
information. You stroll with this intelligence
in and out of fields of knowledge, getting always more
marks on your preserving tablets.

There is another kind of tablet, one
already completed and preserved inside you.
A spring overflowing its springbox. A freshness
in the center of the chest. This other intelligence
does not turn yellow or stagnate. It's fluid,
and it doesn't move from outside to inside
through the conduits of plumbing-learning.

This second knowing is a fountainhead
from within you, moving out.

—*Jellaludin Rumi*

I was sixteen, shifting uncomfortably on my grandmother's small couch. I did not expect to find anything interesting in her bookshelves; there couldn't have been a larger gulf between us. Randomly, I grabbed a book, flipped to the poem "Dialogue." *My god,* I thought, *this is a poem about sex. Right here, in my grandmother's bookshelves.*

"It captures quite a feeling, doesn't it?"

I turned in horror. My grandmother stood behind the loveseat, smiling.

"Yes, yes, it does," I replied.

She turned and walked back into the kitchen. In two sentences, my world changed. This eighty-five-year-old woman, seconds before as alien as another human could be, shattered all age barriers, stereotypes, and formalities. She showed me that my fears and passions and experiences were normal. She helped me discover the power of poetry.

I read this poem twice a year: in the spring on the day she died, and in the late summer to prepare myself for the onslaught of ninth graders. It reminds me how the world looks to a teenager: turned alien overnight. I remember the loneliness and how my grandmother breached the haze and offered the lifeline that only perspective, art, and age can lend.

As a teacher, I find counsel in these memories—they tell me that I am the one who, like my grandmother, must first have the courage to dismantle the comfortable walls of age, experience, and authority.

—*Adam D. Bunting*
High School Administrator
Vermont

Dialogue

She sits with one hand poised against her head, the
other turning an old ring to the light
for hours our talk has beaten
like rain against the screens
a sense of August and heat-lightning
I get up, go to make tea, come back
we look at each other
then she says (and this is what I live through
over and over)—she says: *I do not know*
if sex is an illusion

I do not know
who I was when I did those things
or who I said I was
or whether I willed to feel
what I had read about
or who in fact was there with me
or whether I knew, even then
that there was doubt about these things

—*Adrienne Rich*

"For our next class, I want you to memorize this poem." And she read it aloud, twice, her voice a blessing.

Thus I came to know Galway Kinnell's "St. Francis and the Sow"—as a fearful forty-year-old, taking my first class in writing poems with Marilyn Kallet at the University of Tennessee. Despite my English doctorate, scholarship, and years of teaching, I was a novice at poetry writing, a bud not yet in flower.

I write poems now, and teach others to write them too, along with essays, news stories, and arguments. I know writing's hard. Many resist it—even I don't always love it. But I believe everyone's a writer. We all use language to make sense of ourselves and our worlds, we all have stories worth telling. My teaching of writing springs from an essential affirmation and belief—an affirmation of the writer's self and a belief in the potential for growth.

Kinnell's poem embodies my teaching core. The poem reminds me that all my students can learn: my calling is to "reteach" them their "loveliness." Sometimes this teaching comes through words, as I help a writer see where language and thought catch fire. Sometimes it comes through "touch"—a wordless openness to the silences that hover at the edges of the page. Always it comes through presence to the self and the work.

—Libby Falk Jones
College Professor
Kentucky

Saint Francis and the Sow

The bud
stands for all things,
even for those things that don't flower,
for everything flowers, from within, of self-blessing;
though sometimes it is necessary
to reteach a thing its loveliness,
to put a hand on its brow
of the flower
and retell it in words and in touch
it is lovely
until it flowers again from within, of self-blessing;
as Saint Francis
put his hand on the creased forehead
of the sow, and told her in words and in touch
blessings of earth on the sow, and the sow
began remembering all down her thick length,
from the earthen snout all the way
through the fodder and slops to the spiritual curl of the tail,
from the hard spininess spiked out from the spine
down through the great broken heart
to the sheer blue milken dreaminess spurting and shuddering
from the fourteen teats into the fourteen mouths sucking and
    blowing beneath them:
the long, perfect loveliness of sow.

—*Galway Kinnell*

In my first teaching assignment some of my students were nineteen and twenty years old, while I was only twenty myself. I was no better at keeping order than most new teachers, severely challenged by the students' well-practiced teasing and clowning, doubtful of my legitimacy as enforcer of rules. Fresh from Sunday's protest march, I felt uncomfortable requiring students to keep still on Monday morning. I was touched by their vulnerability and their dependence upon me to know the answers to their questions. My shameful secret was that I didn't know all the answers. In short, I felt I was on the wrong side of the desk.

I wanted to give my students the good news of art and literature, but I was conscious that I would necessarily also deliver bad news; you can hardly appreciate the beauty of life and liberty unless you admit that evil and death loom nearby.

I have returned to Kumin's poem again and again because it embodies a metaphor for this dilemma. The day is bright and warm, the water is beautiful, the obedient students are vulnerable, knees bare, skin exposed. The teacher loves her students and wants for them only what is good, what they need; she's clever enough to devise the activity, pairs playing victim and saver alternately. But the water is perilous and deep, and although the lesson is how to save a life, part of that lesson is that the life saved may be only one's own.

—Thomasina LaGuardia

Retired High School English Teacher
New York

Junior Life Saving

Isosceles of knees
my boys and girls sit
cross-legged in blue July
and finger the peel
of their sun-killed skin
or pick at the splintery boards
of the dock. The old lake
smiles to a fish
and quiets back to glass.

Class, I say, this is
the front head release.
And Adam's boy, whose ribs
dance to be numbered aloud,
I choose to strangle me.
Jaw down in his embrace
I tell the breakaway.
Now swimming in the air
we drown, wrenching the chin,
clawing the arm around.

The magic seeps away.
My heroes frown to see
a menace in the element
they lately loved.
Class, I say (and want
to say, children, my dears,
I too know how to be afraid),
I tell you what I know:
go down to save.

Now two by two they leave
the dock to play at death
by suffocation.
The old lake smiles,
turned sudden to a foe,
taking my children down,
half held by half
ordaining they let go.

—Maxine Kumin

Bishop, California, is a one-high-school town in a one-highway county. Four hours from the nearest metropolis, my students dream about the secret pleasures of big-city life, and the dusty streets echo their wishes. "I will get away," they whisper.

Many want to go to college; all want to get out. The truth is that most stay, and many who leave do not last in a world larger than five thousand people and six traffic lights. Behind the cash registers of the gas stations and the KMart stand these same people, no longer so young, too young to be old.

Each time I reread Gary Soto's "Saturday at the Canal," I am reminded that adolescence is filled with desires and feelings of powerlessness. In Bishop, my students do spend Saturday by the canal—or amid the sage and rabbit brush of the Buttermilks, or engulfed in the noise of two-stroke motorcycle engines at the desert racetrack—imagining a faraway world filled with promise.

Education happens in a context, and my teaching needs to go beyond alliteration, the semicolon, and strong thesis statements. I teach in a world of unfulfilled dreams, so the greatest lessons I can teach are those of survival and resilience. Soto's poem reminds me that when my students leave my classroom, they must know how to read, write, and think critically, but more important, they need to know—in their bones—that the distance to their dreams is not too far from home to travel.

—Steve Elia

High School English Teacher
California

Saturday at the Canal

I was hoping to be happy by seventeen.
School was a sharp check mark in the roll book,
An obnoxious tuba playing at noon because our team
Was going to win at night. The teachers were
Too close to dying to understand. The hallways
Stank of poor grades and unwashed hair. Thus,
A friend and I sat watching the water on Saturday,
Neither of us talking much, just warming ourselves
By hurling large rocks at the dusty ground
And feeling awful because San Francisco was a postcard
On a bedroom wall. We wanted to go there,
Hitchhike under the last migrating birds
And be with people who knew more than three chords
On a guitar. We didn't drink or smoke,
But our hair was shoulder length, wild when
The wind picked up and the shadows of
This loneliness gripped loose dirt. By bus or car,
By the sway of train over a long bridge,
We wanted to get out. The years froze
As we sat on the bank. Our eyes followed the water,
White-tipped but dark underneath, racing out of town.

—*Gary Soto*

Most semesters I find some shimmering moment, even in a class discussing European integration or the difficulty of reconciling democratic transformation with the pressures of globalization, when I excuse myself for a moment, hurry down the hall to my office, and retrieve "Diving into the Wreck" to read aloud.

I teach European politics and political philosophy at Mount Holyoke College. I have taught here more than thirty years—the very best job in the world. It is a profound privilege to spend my days with the gifted young women I teach. Coming from many continents, they bring the world into my office. I am moved by their intense desire to learn, their willingness to explore the world and discover their proper place in it, their sheer pleasure as their world expands exponentially, month after month, and their generosity in sharing their dreams and hopes with me. But it is perhaps the students who are stuck or in deep pain who draw me in most deeply—my work with them is hidden behind my office door, where we sit in two big blue wing chairs and try to find the "next step" in a difficult life.

I read Rich's "Diving into the Wreck" to both groups, because both need to know they are engaged in the most important journey of all: to peer into the darkness and see who they are, where they have come from, and where they might choose to go carrying their own light and message.

—Penny Gill
College Professor
Massachusetts

Diving into the Wreck

First having read the book of myths,
and loaded the camera,
and checked the edge of the knife-blade,
I put on
the body-armor of black rubber
the absurd flippers
the grave and awkward mask.
I am having to do this
not like Cousteau with his
assiduous team
aboard the sun-flooded schooner
but here alone.

There is a ladder.
The ladder is always there
hanging innocently
close to the side of the schooner.
We know what it is for,
we who have used it.
Otherwise
it is a piece of maritime floss
some sundry equipment.

I go down.
Rung after rung and still
the oxygen immerses me
the blue light
the clear atoms
of our human air.

I go down.
My flippers cripple me,
I crawl like an insect down the ladder
and there is no one
to tell me when the ocean
will begin.

First the air is blue and then
it is bluer and then green and then
black I am blacking out and yet
my mask is powerful
it pumps my blood with power
the sea is another story
the sea is not a question of power
I have to learn alone
to turn my body without force
in the deep element.

And now: it is easy to forget
what I came for
among so many who have always
lived here
swaying their crenellated fans
between the reefs
and besides
you breathe differently down here.

I came to explore the wreck.
The words are purposes.

The words are maps.
I came to see the damage that was done
and the treasures that prevail.
I stroke the beam of my lamp
slowly along the flank
of something more permanent
than fish or weed

the thing I came for:
the wreck and not the story of the wreck
the thing itself and not the myth
the drowned face always staring
toward the sun
the evidence of damage
worn by salt and sway into this threadbare
    beauty
the ribs of the disaster
curving their assertion
among the tentative haunters.

This is the place.
And I am here, the mermaid whose dark
    hair
streams black, the merman in his armored
    body
We circle silently
about the wreck
we dive into the hold.
I am she: I am he

whose drowned face sleeps with open eyes
whose breasts still bear the stress
whose silver, copper, vermeil cargo lies
obscurely inside barrels
half-wedged and left to rot
we are the half-destroyed instruments
that once held to a course
the water-eaten log
the fouled compass

We are, I am, you are
by cowardice or courage
the ones who find our way
back to this scene
carrying a knife, a camera
a book of myths
in which
our names do not appear.

—*Adrienne Rich*

The Fire of Teaching

Aclassroom can be a place where world-changing and life-transforming work unfolds as teachers and students come together around the big ideas. It can be a setting where an understanding and tender adult helps steer students through the myriad crags and shoals of growing up. It can be a community of learners where one's imagination can be fired, skills honed, and dreams evoked.

In this section, teachers describe poems that stir them to teach with fire. They describe their drive to push students to seek, explore, and care about ideas. They describe their passion for igniting in students the capacity to understand the connection between ideas in the classroom and the events that transpire in the world outside of school. They describe the thrill of connecting heart-to-heart with students in ways that provoke deep and genuine learning and inspire active engagement with the questions at the center of the subjects we teach.

Teachers with fire are ambitious dreamers and relentless doers who see their work as audacious, bold, and essential.

Discussing issues of inequality is difficult work. Everyone has a personal story about racism and injustice, but some feel anger while others feel guilt. Students who are members of oppressed groups feel resentful when they have to explain racism to white students. Students from privileged backgrounds often feel they are being blamed for the legacy of inequality in America. I have found that using poetry in the college classroom is a powerful tool for bringing new perspectives into the setting. Poets give us a different way of seeing things and allow us to think with our hearts.

This poem speaks to me about humanity and our imperfections. Every semester when I teach a new group of teacher education students about the inequities in our schools, I read this poem and suggest changing the first line to "Out of a hundred families." The response is usually a softening of the hard thoughts of blame and a realization that we are indeed all worthy of compassion.

For me, teaching for social justice is a collaborative practice in which all of the voices in the classroom are valued and affirmed. As an educator, I try to bring those voices out and to learn from them as much as they learn from me. Out of every hundred people—good and bad—black, brown, and white; afraid and in pain; and wise in hindsight—we are all one another's teachers.

—*Elizabeth Meador*

Teacher Educator
California and Colorado

A Contribution to Statistics

Out of a hundred people

Those who always know better
—fifty-two,

doubting every step
—nearly all the rest,

glad to lend a hand
if it doesn't take too long
—as high as forty-nine,

always good,
because they can't be otherwise
—four, well maybe five,

able to admire without envy
—eighteen,

suffering illusions
induced by fleeting youth
—sixty, give or take a few,

not to be taken lightly
—forty and four,

living in constant fear
of someone or something
—seventy-seven,

capable of happiness
—twenty-something tops,

harmless singly,
savage in crowds
—half at least,

cruel
when forced by circumstances
—better not to know
even ballpark figures,

after the fact
—just a couple more
than wise before it,

taking only things from life
—thirty
(I wish I were wrong),

Hunched in pain,
no flashlight in the dark
—eighty-three
sooner or later,

righteous
—thirty-five, which is a lot,

righteous
and understanding
—three,

worthy of compassion
—ninety-nine,

mortal
a hundred out of a hundred.
Thus far this figure still remains
    unchanged.

—Wislawa Szymborska

The only thing I've done longer than teach is, of course, learn. And not very far along it became clear that teaching is learning with others by living into the questions that experience opens.

It was in my second year of teaching—high school, then—that this couplet appeared in my path; it's been a teacher ever since.

> I'd rather learn from one bird how to sing
> than teach ten thousand stars how not to dance

Countless times I've tossed it like a hieroglyph before a class, and just as often I have recited it to myself when puzzled at what to do next.

For in its construction is a telescoped wisdom, very Tao-like, that helps me reunderstand my way in the world:

I'd rather learn . . . than teach. . . .

I'd rather learn from one . . . than teach ten thousand. . . .

And perhaps most important of all: I'd rather learn how to . . . than teach how not to. . . .

In my own journey, I have been worn like a stone shaped by an unending river—from young poet to young teacher to my tumble through cancer to my life as a listener and teacher of the life that lives below all names.

And this chunk of truth continues to remind me that life is a journey from no to yes, and that the classroom appears wherever we dare to imagine this life as a transformative question that we somehow awaken into together.

—*Mark Nepo*
Poet-Teacher
Michigan

You Shall Above All Things

you shall above all things be glad and young.
For if you're young,whatever life you wear

it will become you;and if you are glad
whatever's living will yourself become.
Girlboys may nothing more than boygirls need:
i can entirely her only love

whose any mystery makes every man's
flesh put space on;and his mind take off time

that you should ever think,may god forbid
and(in his mercy)your true lover spare:
for that way knowledge lies,the foetal grave
called progress,and negation's dead undoom.

I'd rather learn from one bird how to sing
than teach ten thousand stars how not to dance

—*E.E. Cummings*

I began to question whether I had wasted my life being a teacher. I had taught in Chicago's inner city, the Virgin Islands, and a university lab school. But for the past twenty-five years, because of family obligations, I'd been in a small suburban school district, far from the fascinating, cutting-edge environments that challenged my heart.

Into this, "The Summer Day" powerfully came asking, "Tell me, what is it you plan to do with your one wild and precious life?" The question hit me like a hammer. The implied answer—that a life can be spent in no better way than in observation, questioning, and celebration of the particular—made me say to myself, "Yes, this is what I have a chance to do every day as I observe my students, read and respond to their writing, listen to their discussions. Teaching invites me into the presence of the precious and wild."

My students enter Advanced Placement English thinking that its primary purpose is to pass the A.P. Test. Sometimes I catch myself thinking that too. Instead, we read this poem and I ask them to answer its question as their first writing assignment. It reminds us that our time together is not only about achieving but also about discovery and being. Their anxiety about grades and class demands lifts as they realize that the essential questions will be the ones they learn to ask themselves. To be present while students pose these questions is my vocation.

—Caren Bassett Dybek
High School English Teacher
Michigan

The Summer Day

Who made the world?
Who made the swan, and the black bear?
Who made the grasshopper?
This grasshopper, I mean—
the one who has flung herself out of the grass,
the one who is eating sugar out of my hand,
who is moving her jaws back and forth instead of up and down—
who is gazing around with her enormous and complicated eyes.
Now she lifts her pale forearms and thoroughly washes her face.
Now she snaps her wings open, and floats away.
I don't know exactly what a prayer is.
I do know how to pay attention, how to fall down
into the grass, how to kneel down in the grass,
how to be idle and blessed, how to stroll through the fields,
which is what I have been doing all day.
Tell me, what else should I have done?
Doesn't everything die at last, and too soon?
Tell me, what is it you plan to do
with your one wild and precious life?

—Mary Oliver

I first read this poem when I was nineteen, and the final line hit me like a thunderbolt. I had to change my life? But how, and what did the headless sculpture of Apollo have to do with this? This dramatic question has accompanied me since that first reading, though I know not exactly what the headless sculpture commands its viewers, or what Rilke urges upon his readers. Change must come from within, even when spurred on from the outside.

I believe that Rilke's poem embodies the very essence of transformative teaching, the goal that education brings about a change in someone's life, a change that can alter students at their cores. This is as true of the elementary school teacher as of the college professor. What teacher goes into education aspiring merely to increase the skills of students, to raise their test scores? Not many, I'd wager.

In addition to conveying skills and raising scores, transformative teachers silently exhort students to imagine what is not visible, to nurture what passions burn within them. These teachers secretly hope that the effect of their presence in the classroom will be that of Rilke's poem: the instruction to change your life, to see the world with fresh eyes, to become something new.

This poem reminds me every time I read it that art can indeed transform human beings, and that teaching is its own art form with the same potential end.

—Rob Reich

College Professor
California

Archaic Torso of Apollo

We cannot know his legendary head
with eyes like ripening fruit. And yet his torso
is still suffused with brilliance from inside,
like a lamp, in which his gaze, now turned to low,

gleams in all its power. Otherwise
the curved breast could not dazzle you so, nor could
a smile run through the placid hips and thighs
to that dark center where procreation flared.

Otherwise this stone would seem defaced
beneath the translucent cascade of the shoulders
and would not glisten like a wild beast's fur:

would not, from all the borders of itself,
burst like a star: for here there is no place
that does not see you. You must change your life.

—*Ranier Maria Rilke*

Boxes. Neatly tied parcels that categorize and organize the world are handy for creating an illusion of tidy happiness, but in actuality, these borders limit perspective and possibility. "Dare to think": the words fuel my revolutionary vehicle. Thinking critically is essential in a world so full of influences. Yet how many students have learned not to think and instead continually seek the easy way out? I have witnessed how the educational system can push students away from learning and understanding, even discourage thinking. The root of the problem reaches beyond school. The media wash young brains so clean that the fibers no longer cling together. Their energy replaced by fixed images and ideas, they leave brain parts dangling into empty space. Thinking? That's too hard.

My work begins as I examine the faces around the table. "Why are you here?" I ask. My heart sinks, though I know the answers well enough: "I have to be." "My parents made me." "It's a requirement."

"OK, but why are *you* here?" Pens and pencils scratch the paper, digging for answers, for understanding. I dare students to think critically, recognize their internal power, and break free from boxes that create artificial order and real injustice. Inevitably I meet resistance, as habit is the enemy of change. But I know that if students can see beyond their boxes and understand the "greatness, rareness, muchness / Fewness of this precious only / Endless world in which they live," then they can dare to live.

—Ali Stewart

Middle School Art Teacher
Germany

Warning to Children

Children, if you dare to think
Of the greatness, rareness, muchness
Fewness of this precious only
Endless world in which you say
You live, you think of things like this:
Blocks of slate enclosing dappled
Red and green, enclosing tawny
Yellow nets, enclosing white
And black acres of dominoes,
Where a neat brown paper parcel
Tempts you to untie the string.
In the parcel a small island,
On the island a large tree,
On the tree a husky fruit.
Strip the husk and pare the rind off:
In the kernel you will see
Blocks of slate enclosed by dappled
Red and green, enclosed by tawny
Yellow nets, enclosed by white
And black acres of dominoes,
Where the same brown paper parcel—
Children, leave the string untied!
For who dares undo the parcel
Finds himself at once inside it,
On the island, in the fruit,
Blocks of slate about his head,

Finds himself enclosed by dappled
Green and red, enclosed by yellow
Tawny nets, enclosed by black
And white acres of dominoes,
With the same brown paper parcel
Still untied upon his knee.
And, if he then should dare to think
Of the fewness, muchness, rareness,
Greatness of this endless only
Precious world in which he says
He lives—he then unties the string.

—*Robert Graves*

Wallace Stevens writes the kind of poems that I would write if only I could find the words. Stevens is both a visionary and a comedian and for me that's a wonderful combination. One lyric that I particularly admire is "The Poem That Took the Place of a Mountain." I have read Stevens's poetry throughout my adult life, but I somehow missed this dazzler until a few years ago. Quite appropriately, I first read it during a camping trip in the Berkshires. It is a poem about the exhilaration of reading poetry and compares the mind in the act of exploring a great poem to a mountain climber making his way up a mountain.

When I teach the poem, my students and I read it out loud several times to emphasize its playfulness and internalize its rhythms. One of the amazing things about this lyric is that its metrical momentum regulates our breath and makes us feel as if we were following the climber up the slope, stepping up on the imagination toward truth. The reward for all this effort, both intellectual and physical, is a new perspective on the world and a deeper understanding of what it means to be human. Every time I read the poem, I feel like I am back in the Berkshires; and for a moment at least, the air tastes fresh and cold and clean.

—Samuel Scheer

High School English Teacher
Connecticut

The Poem That Took the Place of a Mountain

There it was, word for word,
The poem that took the place of a mountain.

He breathed its oxygen,
Even when the book lay turned in the dust of his table.

It reminded him how he had needed
A place to go to in his own direction,

How he had recomposed the pines,
Shifted the rocks and picked his way among clouds,

For the outlook that would be right,
Where he would be complete in an unexplained completion:

The exact rock where his inexactness
Would discover, at last, the view toward which they had edged,

Where he could lie and, gazing down at the sea,
Recognize his unique and solitary home.

—*Wallace Stevens*

Visiting my middle school English teachers recently, I realized how important it is to have teachers who are passionate about poetry. They didn't just teach me a skill; they gave me a gift, a way to see and make sense of the world. Thirty years later, that gift is as rich, vibrant, and exciting as ever. Without it, how could I live?

With these teachers in mind, I bring poetry into my classroom. Last year, I read from *The Palm of My Heart,* a collection of poetry by African American children. A white student said he felt put down or left out by a poem on the beauty of black hands. If the poem did not say that white hands were also beautiful, he reasoned, maybe the poet was saying they were ugly. The class considered how people with dark skin might feel when reading poems about white people. We talked about whether the poet should have to include white people in her poem, if what she really wants to talk about are her hands and the hands in her family.

We turned to "My People." I love how this poem helps my students see from new perspectives and develop questioning habits of mind, such as What is beauty? Who are my people? A poem may be beautiful or not, but each poem is a way of seeing and making sense of the world. By sharing my passion for poetry, I hope to nurture my students' hunger for their own voices and those of others.

—*Mary Cowhey*
First-Grade Teacher
Massachusetts

My People

The night is beautiful,
So the faces of my people.

The stars are beautiful,
So the eyes of my people.

Beautiful, also, is the sun.
Beautiful, also, are the souls of my people.

—Langston Hughes

When I was twelve, my mother would leave me at the public library where I could lie on the floor of the children's section surrounded by my favorite things—words. I remember vividly the day I pulled out a book that opened to "the drum." I learned right then that a poem didn't have to rhyme or have proper punctuation or capitalization. I learned right then that I was a poet—no matter what my teachers and the textbooks said.

In high school, I decorated my bedroom wall with "the drum" in large black letters cut from magazines: a ransom note to remind me not to lose my soul despite troubles at home and in my heart. In college, I brought it to life as a homemade drum painted like the world. Alone in my dorm room, I beat out rhythms, trying to figure out who I wanted to be.

Now, an educator and mentor, I carry copies of this six-line poem typed onto business-size cards and give them to young people I meet. Something usually tells me that someone in their life was like my father, a man whose greatest line of comfort was "get used to it, life isn't fair." I hand these words to young people in hopes that they, too, will grow to understand that no matter how unfair life can be, they always have the opportunity to add something to the world that is beautiful, because it is uniquely their own.

—Sam Grabelle
Education Administrator
Rhode Island

the drum

daddy says the world
is a drum tight
and hard
and i told him
i'm gonna beat out
my own rhythm

—*nikki giovanni*

We spend a great deal of time in sixth grade seeking to understand our nation's history. All too often it comes to us with much that is missing or changed. I believe it is our responsibility as teachers to challenge the distortions and lies, to make sure that our students see the whole story, what really happened and how it affects us all. Correctives are required. As the African proverb says, "Until the lion tells the tale, stories of the hunt will tend to glorify the hunter."

nila northSun, a Native American, provides a straightforward documentation of what has been lost. The poem goes a long way toward enlightening students about a people's and culture's struggle to maintain its connection to its history, its roots, its identity. The poem is about the experience of Native Americans, but it is also about what many cultures have paid and continue to pay as the price of membership. And it is about how we all have been impoverished by these losses.

Poems like this help me to challenge students to enter into another's experience and to bring alive the many sides and aspects of our history. To look at times when we too may "dance to the music." Each year, the quiet epiphanies experienced as we discuss the deeper meaning of the poem remind me of why I became a teacher.

—Tom Weiner
Sixth-Grade Teacher
Massachusetts

moving camp too far

i can't speak of
    many moons
    moving camp on travois
i can't tell of
    the last great battle
    counting coups or
    taking scalps
i don't know what it
    was to hunt buffalo
    or do the ghost dance
but
i can see an eagle
    almost extinct
    on slurpee plastic cups
i can travel to powwows
    in campers & winnebagos
i can eat buffalo meat
    at the tourist burger stand
i can dance to indian music
    rock-n-roll hey-a-hey-o
i can
    & unfortunately
    i do.

                    —nila northSun

I asked students to watch a video of Milosz reciting "Gift" in Polish and English. Initially, many described it as sad. Part of that was probably the softness of Milosz's voice, and I suspect part was a result of the overwhelmingly somber themes in literature we ask students to consider in school. Then we watched the clip over and over and wrote the lines until everyone had it. The repetition worked. Almost immediately they saw the poem as expansive and hopeful, and easily committed it to memory. When asked to write their own "Perfect Day" poem in response, they were eager to try.

For weeks afterward, students would shuffle into class saying, "A day so happy," in their best Milosz imitation and then crack up. The following semester, when I repeated the exercise, a few started laughing wildly. "So that's why our friends kept saying 'a day so happy' at the oddest times!"

To me, this poem is a pause that pulls me to revisit who I am. It expresses simple pleasures. "Gift" helps me, and students, consider what we value. I believe being a teacher is about encouraging students to think about and clarify what they know and believe about themselves and the world. This exploration is what propels lifelong curiosity. Poetry is a way for me to connect to others, and "Gift," in particular, helps me share who I am with teenagers.

—Suzanne Strauss

High School English Teacher
Massachusetts

Gift

A day so happy.
Fog lifted early, I worked in the garden.
Hummingbirds were stopping over honeysuckle flowers.
There was no thing on earth I wanted to possess.
I knew no one worth my envying him.
Whatever evil I had suffered, I forgot.
To think that once I was the same man did not embarrass me.
In my body I felt no pain.
When straightening up, I saw the blue sea and sails.

—Czeslaw Milosz

For over thirty years I have been an English and literacy teacher in Boston high schools. So much talk in urban schools revolves around the language of our students, often decried as deficient. I have heard teachers suggest that the language, parents, and culture of students result in their lacking the ability to talk and write well. I have often heard the complaint: "Students cannot write; they cannot write a coherent, correct sentence."

I turn and return to Eliot's words, pasted above me at school, because he tells me that meaning and language are hard work for all of us. His words remind me that every student's struggle—every human's struggle—is to marry meaning to language and language to meaning. And this is not easy for all of us who are "trying to learn to use words" that equal our transient realties, which include our "mess of imprecision of feeling." All of us who speak and write use "shabby equipment always deteriorating."

No language or culture should try to prevent the liberating struggle that acknowledges naming as power. Classrooms and schools must be places that encourage students and teachers to talk and write to name their individual and cultural experience without censure and reproof. For as Eliot says, we will "get the better of words" only in that moment when our words fill the room or page. For us, as teachers, we must hold the space for "only the trying. The rest is not our business."

—Stephen Gordon
High School Literacy Teacher
Massachusetts

East Coker

So here I am, in the middle way, having had twenty years—
Twenty years largely wasted, the years of *l'entre deux guerres*
Trying to learn to use words, and every attempt
Is a wholly new start, and a different kind of failure
Because one has only learnt to get the better of words
For the thing one no longer has to say, or the way in which
One is no longer disposed to say it. And so each venture
Is a new beginning, a raid on the inarticulate
With shabby equipment always deteriorating
In the general mess of imprecision of feeling,
Undisciplined squads of emotion. And what there is to conquer
By strength and submission, has already been discovered
Once or twice, or several times, by men whom one cannot hope
To emulate—but there is no competition—
There is only the fight to recover what has been lost
And found and lost again and again: and now, under conditions
That seem unpropitious. But perhaps neither gain nor loss.
For us, there is only the trying. The rest is not our business.

—*T. S. Eliot*

Simple and straightforward, this poem captures a moment of focused attention and care between a father and young son. The poem also gives voice to a larger reality in our world: our interdependence.

I have shared this poem with many teachers but most memorably at a teacher renewal retreat in Singapore. As one of two Americans working with thirty teachers of Chinese, Malay, and Indian descent and of Muslim, Buddhist, Christian, and Hindu faiths, I was amazed by how this simple poem helped us penetrate the walls that divided us.

As one teacher, himself a devout Muslim, said, "Because we took the time to get to know one another and to hear each other's stories and passion for teaching, I leave here more tolerant."

Our multiple roles and realities merged in a moment of grace when we recognized that we share common dreams for the children entrusted to us. While we may not know the contents of the boy's dream as he lay on his father's shoulder, each of us could easily imagine the dreams of this father for his young son—that he grow up healthy and whole, get a good education, find work, create a home, and live in a world where peace is practiced and conflict is resolved without violence. In that moment we understood the fragile truth in the poet's words, "we're not going to be able to live in this world if we're not willing to do what he's doing with one another."

—Marcy Jackson
Co-Director, Center for Courage & Renewal
Washington

Shoulders

A man crosses the street in rain,
stepping gently, looking two times north and south,
because his son is asleep on his shoulder.

No car must splash him.
No car drive too near to his shadow.

This man carries the world's most sensitive cargo
but he's not marked.
Nowhere does his jacket say FRAGILE,
HANDLE WITH CARE.

His ear fills up with breathing.
He hears the hum of a boy's dream
deep inside him.

We're not going to be able
to live in this world
if we're not willing to do what he's doing
with one another.

The road will only be wide.
The rain will never stop falling.

—*Naomi Shihab Nye*

It is going to be a bad meeting, this so-called "staff development." The out-of-town expert is at the podium preparing to tell us how *we should* be doing *our* work.

Often, that "expert" is me. Like many educators, I must struggle to keep my audience engaged. If I don't meaningfully connect, I not only fail to be helpful but also exacerbate their despair. So, after the introduction, I pass out this poem on brightly colored paper and read it aloud. The assignment is simple: turn to the person next to you and identify one phrase that somehow moved you.

After a pause that invokes Tina Turner (What's *poetry* got to do with it?) the room never fails to come alive. This poem brings young people spilling into the room; it reconnects educators to their deepest vocational and often spiritual longings; it puts race and gender and change squarely on the table, while looking beyond all three; it reminds us of the developmental nature of education and challenges us to see how far we've strayed from the ideal.

Then I ask them how the process of school improvement could be more like the interpretation of a poem than the following of a blueprint. What if school reform needs the work of a skilled gardener rather than engineer? How would we proceed if we had to agree on one right meaning to situations as complex and evocative as this poem? Then, after a moment's rich silence, the real conversation begins.

—Linda Powell Pruitt
Organizational Consultant
New York

Harvest Home

In the ideal
it is a harvesting,
this work we do—
a reaping of crops grown
from ancestral seeds,
a gathering of first fruit
from vines that trace their sources
    beyond geography,
    beyond gender,
    beyond the bleach
      and blush
         and black of skin
and root themselves in watery grace,
in knowledge that nurtures us all.

In the ideal
our classrooms fill, like cornucopia,
overflowing with the bounty of our grange.
Life stories, heaped among the texts,
spill into hallways of our schools,
crowd the sidewalks or the subways
or ride yellow buses home,
altering the form of knowing,
changing heads,
    changing hearts,
      changing history,
bringing harvest
home.

                —*Bettye T. Spinner*

Daring to Lead

*M*ovements begin when individuals dare to act on their deepest convictions. It takes a special strength and a willingness to withstand and stand with pain, criticism, and disappointment and actively resist the relentless force of an institution as intractable as school. However, those who dare to stand tall slowly discover others who share their vision.

The poems in this section stir teachers to consider their own journey in the movement to make schools more humane, just, and inspired settings. These teachers describe their decision to stand tall against those forces that undermine what they value. They describe the exhilaration of discovering common cause with fellow teachers and they invite us all to imagine what schools would be like if they were recreated to be caring and invigorating places for teachers, administrators, and students to work and to learn. It will take courageous individuals daring to stand tall side-by-side to make this happen.

Most people become teachers because they loved their time in school and don't want to leave. A few become teachers because school was so damaging they don't want to see the same hurts happen to more children. I was that other kind of English teacher.

I hated school—especially high school. For a long time, I didn't know why. I loved reading, learning, and talking about important questions. But that's not what we did in school. We mostly sat and listened and spat back the teachers' ideas. Meanwhile, the world was more and more confusing—I went to church where they preached about love but then snarled viciously when someone mentioned blacks coming to my school. On TV, I saw people—children sometimes—chased by dogs, beaten by police. Then we nearly blew up the world—for what? And the time they shot the president—why?

Growing up, the world made no sense to me. In twelfth grade, I started reading aphorisms and wrote one that summed up my experience of school: "Is life nothing more than a question and answer period, where the questions go unanswered, and the answers go unquestioned?" Eventually my readings led me to Paul Goodman's *Growing Up Absurd* and to *Summerhill* by A. S. Neil. Both helped me see that school could be very different. But Tagore's poem, discovered years later, best answers "What's school really for, anyway?" This poem is a prayer that calls for the relentless search for Truth, without limitations.

—Tony Wagner

Co-Director, Change Leadership Group
Massachusetts

Where the Mind Is Without Fear

Where the mind is without fear and the head is held high;

Where knowledge is free;

Where the world has not been broken up into fragments by narrow domestic walls;

Where words come out from the depth of truth;

Where tireless striving stretches its arms towards perfection;

Where the clear stream of reason has not lost its way into the dreary desert sand of dead habit;

Where the mind is led forward by thee into ever-widening thought and action—

Into that heaven of freedom, my Father, let my country awake.

—*Rabindranath Tagore*

Barbara Kingsolver describes hearing on her kitchen radio that the state board of education was dropping the poetry requirement for Arizona schools. *The secretary of education explained that it takes too much time to teach children poetry, when they are harder pressed than ever to master the essentials of the curriculum. He said that we have to take a good, hard look at what is essential, and what is superfluous.*

Indeed.

Are Arizona's schools doing better since that 1997 decision? (I looked it up. Not a bit.) Yet pressure is growing everywhere to eliminate "frills" a la Arizona.

Poetry occupies a big, essential space in the life and learning of our youth. Kids are creating, memorizing, recording, and performing poetry, publishing 'zines, slamming and rapping and rhyming and relishing poetry, but rarely in the classroom. Poetry is a force of nature. You can drive its rhythms out of school, but they emerge, more powerful, in the streets and souls of the young.

What we choose not to teach is as important as what we choose to teach. What does it say about our democracy when we silence Walt Whitman telling us, "I hear America singing, the varied carols I hear," or Langston Hughes reminding us, "I am the darker brother," or the newest, high-energy hiphop poets, whose voices wake up our students?

To paraphrase the classic bumper sticker: When poetry is outlawed, only outlaws will be poets. Perhaps that includes teachers and students. At least in Arizona.

—Susan Klonsky

Associate Director, Small Schools Workshop
Illinois

Beating Time

Commemorating the removal of poetry as a requirement in Arizona's schools, August 1997

The Governor interdicted: poetry is evicted
from our curricula,
for metaphor and rhyme take time
from science. Our children's self-reliance rests
upon the things we count on. The laws
of engineering. Poeteering squanders time, and time
is money. He said: let the chips fall where they may.

The Governor's voice fell down through quicksilver
microchip song hummed along and the law
was delivered to its hearing. The students
of engineering bent to their numbers in silent
classrooms, where the fans overhead
whispered "I am I am" in iambic pentameter.
Unruly and fractious numbers were discarded at the bell.
In the crumpled, cast-off equations,
small black figures shaped like tadpoles
formed a nation, unobserved, in the wastepaper basket.

Outside, a storm is about to crack the sky.
Lightning will score dry riverbeds, peeling back the mud
like a plow, bellowing, taking out bridges,
completely unexpectedly.

The children too young to have heard
of poetry's demise turn their eyes
to the windows, to see what they can count on.
They will rise and dance to the iamb of the fans,
whispering illicit rhymes,
watching the sky for a sign
while the rain beats time.

—*Barbara Kingsolver*

If poetry is the simple expression of a complex sentiment, arranging words to give both balance and force to an important idea and asserting a principle that transcends its rhetoric, then this sentence by Thomas Jefferson is poetry.

By conventional standards it is a labored sentence, wordy, convoluted, and likely to attract the red pen of a literal-minded English teacher. A closer reading, however, especially aloud, finds it to be a spare expression of the most fundamental principle upon which public education in a democracy rests. The *people* are the truest *depository* of *power;* and if the people are ill equipped to exercise their *control* over that power, then a wise government will *inform their discretion.*

It makes a leap of faith, confident in the power of the human mind and believing in the fairness—the discretion—of an informed heart. It summons us as well: We teachers are to provoke and value that discretion. It has always appealed to me, particularly after an argument with confident critics of schools—the ones whose contempt of school people is barely hidden and whose patience is short with teachers who wish to "inform" the "discretion" of young people rather than briskly giving them the answers to everything.

My wife, Nancy, who has often welcomed me home after such confrontations, penned it on paperboard, framed it, and gave it to me for my office. It has hung there for years now, a reminder of what education in a democracy can and should and must be.

—Theodore R. Sizer

Founder, Coalition for Essential Schools
Massachusetts

Passage from a Letter to William Charles Jarvis, September 28, 1820

I know no safe depository of the ultimate powers of the society but the people themselves; and if we think them not enlightened enough to exercise their control with a wholesome discretion, the remedy is not to take it from them, but to inform their discretion.

—*Thomas Jefferson*

Style is a serious word. It connotes how you do everything in your personal and professional life. As Coco Chanel—whom Jean Cocteau called the "Picasso of fashion"—remarked, *"la mode change, le style rest"* (fashion changes, style remains). The difference is telling: fashion is imposed from without while style is created from within. Fashion demands unthinking subordination and style springs from self-awareness and individual expression.

"Delight in Disorder," is a paean to feminine charm and personal style. The poet describes how his beloved lady dresses and the impact of her appearance on his emotions. Her seeming disarray arouses his desire, expressed in words like "enthralls," "tempestuous," and the wonderful oxymoron "wild civility." This disheveled demeanor is to him more bewitching in a woman than "when art is too precise in every part."

This poem, seemingly superficial and perhaps silly, has a deeper meaning for me. If Chanel is right, teachers today should be skeptical of pedagogical fads and educational reforms. Socrates had no textbooks, used no chalkboards, gave no homework. His tests were not standardized but individualized, challenging each student to question anything, define everything, and measure all things by reason. Teachers could find no better model for excellence.

I believe that effective teaching is an expression of personality—the prism through which character is refracted. The challenge in the classroom is to integrate the content of the curriculum with the content of character. Discovering and developing a personal style is the essence of sound teaching and successful learning.

—Edward Alan Katz
Middle School English Teacher
New York

Delight in Disorder

A sweet disorder in the dress
Kindles in clothes a wantonness:
A lawn about the shoulders thrown
Into a fine distraction,
An erring lace, which here and there
Enthrals the crimson stomacher,
A cuff neglectful, and thereby
Ribbands to flow confusedly,
A winning wave (deserving note)
In the tempestuous petticoat,
A careless shoe-string, in whose tie
I see a wild civility,
Do more bewitch me, than when art
Is too precise in every part.

—*Robert Herrick*

We want to lift and speed a movement—an effort of thousands taking many shapes, an effort to create effective and humane learning environments that prepare young people for the world they will inherit.

Like Rilke, we hope that this movement will be larger than we dare imagine. Our efforts are small compared to the challenge but complemented by legions working in large and small ways to speak truth, do justice, and show kindness. Spirited teachers, inspiring principals and deans, visionary system heads—they are the leaders of this movement.

Parker Palmer and I believe that leadership can be taught, or at least caught. It begins with a heart for service, an opening to the needs around you. Sometimes that opening is a poem. Sometimes it's a parent. My father showed me the needs in our community by bringing me to inner-city ministries every week. He taught me by example that it was our responsibility to serve those less fortunate. My father continues to fight for health care for the poor against enormous odds, facing repeated defeat. He'll die fighting.

I want to live like that—to live fighting for poor African American and Hispanic young people who won't graduate from high school or have a chance to go to college. It is the most important civic, social, and economic fight of our day. I want to be part of creating life-giving learning places, schools that inspire, care, lift, and celebrate; that seek to free what waits within every child.

—*Tom Vander Ark*

Executive Director, Education, Bill and Melinda Gates Foundation
Washington

Teaching with Fire

I Believe in All That Has Never Yet Been Spoken

I believe in all that has never yet been spoken.
I want to free what waits within me
so that what no one has dared to wish for

may for once spring clear
without my contriving.

If this is arrogant, God, forgive me,
but this is what I need to say.
May what I do flow from me like a river,
no forcing and no holding back,
the way it is with children.

Then in these swelling and ebbing currents,
these deepening tides moving out, returning,
I will sing you as no one ever has,

streaming through widening channels
into the open sea.

—Rainer Maria Rilke

A proud black woman recited this poem to me as we marched through the streets of Wichita in 1965. I was scared. We were in the city's first major civil rights demonstration. People were screaming at us. Some were throwing bottles or bricks.

The woman next to me noticed that I was frightened. She asked me how old I was. "Sixteen," I replied.

She asked if I'd ever heard the terrible things people were yelling at us. "No," I answered." She explained that she had heard such insults all her life.

Then, as we continued walking, she recited Langston Hughes's magnificent "Mother to Son." That extraordinary poem made me calmer, more focused, and more determined.

For decades, when I've been discouraged by the slow pace of change, by the resistance of some people, by the difficulty of making reforms that seem so obvious, I've reread "Mother to Son." The poem isn't just about courage. It's also a reminder that all our efforts build on those of people who came along before we did. It's helped me, as an inner-city teacher, administrator, parent, and reform advocate, learn from others who came before.

The poem also praises persistence. It reminds me that many people struggled, often without generous foundation grants, publicity, or political support that we have now.

They kept "a-climbin' on, reaching landin's, turnin' corners, And sometimes going in the dark." We should honor their brave work by continuing it.

—Joe Nathan
Director, Center for School Change
Minnesota

Mother to Son

Well, son, I'll tell you:
Life for me ain't been no crystal stair.
It's had tacks in it,
And splinters,
And boards torn up,
And places with no carpet on the floor—
Bare.
But all the time
I'se been a-climbin' on,
And reachin' landin's,
And turnin' corners,
And sometimes goin' in the dark
Where there ain't been no light.
So boy, don't you turn back.
Don't you set down on the steps
'Cause you finds it's kinder hard.
Don't you fall now—
For I'se still goin', honey,
I'se still climbin',
And life for me ain't been no crystal stair.

—Langston Hughes

It was during my college years in the early 1970s that I first heard the melodious voice of nikki giovanni. Her body was dwarfed by the podium that held her papers, but she stood tall as she unfolded the powerful words of "ego-tripping" to an audience hushed in awe. My spirit soared as she proclaimed the greatness of a people often held in disdain as though their very existence was born of a curse spewed at the beginning of time. I sat up straighter and straighter as each new phrase was given its proper air time.

I was an African American student on a campus that was majority White. Like many others, I had often found myself in this situation. Though I had known of the great contributions that Americans of African descent had made to this nation, that contribution was rarely acknowledged during my schooling. To hear "ego-tripping" in this space, surrounded by students, faculty, and community members of all races and cultures, brought a renewed hope that Africa's greatness could be captured for all to see and cherish.

I began my career teaching in a Catholic elementary school in the heart of Milwaukee's central city. I made a commitment to steep my students in the literary works of African Americans. I wanted them to hold these works in their heads and hearts as armor against the cruelties of a world wounded by hatred.

—Janice E. Jackson

Teacher Educator
Massachusetts

ego-tripping
(there may be a reason why)

I was born in the congo
I walked to the fertile crescent and built
   the sphinx
I designed a pyramid so tough that a star
   that only glows every one hundred years falls
   into the center giving divine perfect light
I am bad

I sat on the throne
   drinking nectar with allah
I got hot and sent an ice age to europe
   to cool my thirst
My oldest daughter is nefertiti
   the tears from my birth pains
   created the nile
I am a beautiful woman

I gazed on the forest and burned
   out the sahara desert
   with a packet of goat's meat
   and a change of clothes
I crossed it in two hours
I am a gazelle so swift
   so swift you can't catch me

   For a birthday present when he was three
I gave my son hannibal an elephant
   He gave me rome for mother's day
My strength flows ever on

My son noah built new/ark and
I stood proudly at the helm
   as we sailed on a soft summer day
I turned myself into myself and was
   jesus
   men intone my loving name
   All praises All praises
I am the one who would save

I sowed diamonds in my back yard
My bowels deliver uranium
   the filings from my fingernails are
   semi-precious jewels
   On a trip north
I caught a cold and blew
My nose giving oil to the arab world
I am so hip even my errors are correct
I sailed west to reach east and had to round off
   the earth as I went
   The hair from my head thinned and gold
    was laid
   across three continents

I am so perfect so divine so ethereal so surreal
I cannot be comprehended
   except by my permission

I mean . . . I . . . can fly
   like a bird in the sky . . .

—nikki giovanni

It was the part about riding a bike that first grabbed me. This was a poem about *courage,* and Anne Sexton used learning to ride a bike as an example of the small things in which we see it. I remember the terror I felt holding fiercely to the handlebars, my legs tottering as I struggled to grip the pedals. No one else seemed to be afraid but me. So I liked it that Sexton saw in my moment of ordinary triumph an act of courage.

I want my students to read that first stanza, to recognize their courageous selves in the everyday of childhood. I want them to understand that the strength, beauty, and dignity of a soldier's courage stems from those small things, those simple acts of life. I want them to trust that love can be there and that courage can sustain them. I want them, my students, my kinsmen, to know they can endure.

We teachers stand before our students, guiding their learning in more ways than we often articulate. Times come when the community of us, students and teachers, are powdered in sorrow. Times come when I have needed to take a deep breath in order to stand before my students, anchored in resolve, swallowing that small coal, believing in the wings of roses. I like to think that they have recognized my small displays of courage. I like to think that, when they do, they believe in their own courageous selves.

—*Wendy Kohler*
Curriculum Director
Massachusetts

Courage

It is in the small things we see it.
The child's first step,
as awesome as an earthquake.
The first time you rode a bike,
wallowing up the sidewalk.
The first spanking when your heart
went on a journey all alone.
When they called you crybaby
or poor or fatty or crazy
and made you into an alien,
you drank their acid
and concealed it.

Later,
if you faced the death of bombs and bullets
you did not do it with a banner,
you did it with only a hat to
cover your heart.
You did not fondle the weakness inside you
though it was there.
Your courage was a small coal
that you kept swallowing.
If your buddy saved you
and died himself in so doing,
then his courage was not courage,
it was love; love as simple as shaving soap.

Later,
if you have endured a great despair,
then you did it alone
getting a transfusion from the fire,
picking the scabs off your heart,
then wringing it out like a sock.
Next, my kinsman, you powdered your
    sorrow,
you gave it a back rub
and then you covered it with a blanket
and after it had slept a while
it woke to the wings of the roses
and was transformed.

Later,
when you face old age and its natural
    conclusion
your courage will still be shown in the
    little ways,
each spring will be a sword you'll sharpen,
those you love will live in a fever of love,
and you'll bargain with the calendar
and at the last moment
when death opens the back door
you'll put on your carpet slippers
and stride out.

—Anne Sexton

My leadership roles in education have taught me the importance of self-knowledge and the grace that accompanies being comfortable in one's own skin. In our rush to "fix" the so-called educational crisis in our schools and universities, many of us have come to realize that our best efforts are doomed if we fail to cherish, challenge, and nurture the human heart that is the very source of effective leadership. I have long used poetry as a means to deepen conversations and connect with my own inner life.

I first came to fully appreciate "Silver Star" during a hard time in my professional life. I had made a series of difficult and controversial decisions. I felt isolated and removed from my colleagues—my first real sense of loneliness. I also struggled with my colleagues' suffering as a result of my actions. "Silver Star" was a gift at just the right time. I felt like Stafford's mountain: "To be a mountain you have to climb alone and accept all that rain and snow."

We often have to navigate the forces at play in our lives and institutions. When I use "Silver Star" in meetings with other leaders, we unpack the poem in small groups as a way to get at the hard truths of leadership and the education profession. The poem enables us to encounter the deeper issues before us and gives us courage when we feel the need to "stand against the wind."

—Jay Casbon
College President
Oregon

Silver Star

To be a mountain you have to climb alone
and accept all that rain and snow. You have to look
far away when evening comes. If a forest
grows, you care; you stand there leaning against
the wind, waiting for someone with faith enough
to ask you to move. Great stones will tumble
against each other and gouge your sides. A storm
will live somewhere in your canyons hoarding its lightning.

If you are lucky, people will give you a dignified
name and bring crowds to admire how sturdy you are,
how long you can hold still for the camera. And some time,
they say, if you last long enough you will hear God;
a voice will roll down from the sky and all your patience
will be rewarded. The whole world will hear it: "Well done."

—*William Stafford*

When the Twin Towers were built, I resented their bold intrusion, dwarfing my beloved Woolworth tower and other landmarks. Then I grew to love them, too. Now my heart aches every time I approach Manhattan. I think of a sign in one of the memorials that sprang up after they fell: "There is a hole in my city and a hole in my heart."

Feeling this same hole, I turned to Walt Whitman's poetry for solace, energy, and affirmation. When I read him about Brooklyn and Manhattan and teeming multitudes and battles real and virtual, I am reminded of something simple: life goes on. It goes on in reality, in flesh, in spirit, in imagination.

Perhaps it's because I grew up in Brooklyn and crossed so often into Manhattan that I return over and over to "Crossing Brooklyn Ferry." I remember the very first time I saw that majestic view, when I was about seven years old and the train emerged from the tunnel. My heart jumped at the sight, and I fell in love forever.

I go back to this poem because it reminds me that the skyline is ever changing, but the life, vibrancy, beauty, and humanity of the city continues. It is that belief in the strength and humanity of our people and our country that inspires my work as an educator and leader. Whitman's zest, his enthusiasm for the freedom and beauty of our land, our cities, our men and women and children, helps sustain it.

—Sandra Feldman

President, American Federation of Teachers
New York

From "Crossing Brooklyn Ferry"

Flood-tide below me! I see you face to face!
Clouds of the west—sun there half an hour high—I see you also face to face.

Crowds of men and women attired in the usual costumes, how curious you are to me!
On the ferry-boats the hundreds and hundreds that cross, returning home, are
    more curious to me than you suppose,
And you that shall cross from shore to shore years hence are more to me, and
    more in my meditations, than you might suppose. . . .
Others will enter the gates of the ferry and cross from shore to shore,
Others will watch the run of the flood-tide,
Others will see the shipping of Manhattan north and west, and the heights of
    Brooklyn to the south and east,
Others will see the islands large and small;
Fifty years hence, others will see them as they cross, the sun half and hour high,
A hundred years hence, or ever so many hundred years hence, others will see them,
Will enjoy the sunset, the pouring-in of the flood-tide, the falling-back to the
    sea of the ebb-tide.

It avails not, time nor place—distance avails not,
I am with you, you men and women of a generation, or ever so many generations
    hence,
Just as you feel when you look on the river and sky, so I felt,
Just as any of you is one of a living crowd, I was one of a crowd, . . .

—*Walt Whitman*

In the days immediately following 9/11, statesman, dissident, and playwright Vaclav Havel seemed so right when much else seemed so wrong. Time stood still for a brief interval after the brutal attack, as though the hijacked airliners had torn the fabric of history. Those early days opened a hiatus in which we had a brief moment to choose the kind of future we wanted for ourselves and our children, the future we would create for our country in a world even more radically interdependent than any of us had perceived it to be.

Our choice amid the stillness of the shock and the grief was how would we move on. Would we respond to the terrible assault with anger, hatred, and more violence; or would we find a viable way—some new way not fully imaginable—to restore our sense of safety, and preserve our precious democratic experiment, with compassion, nonviolence, and love?

The window closed, history resumed, and we chose the violent path. But Havel's words remain for us, as we seek to rebuild. The "salvation of this human world," Havel once said to the U.S. Congress, "lies nowhere else than in the human heart, in the human power to reflect, in human meekness and in human responsibility." All is not lost if we will resist the forces that conspire to disabuse us of what we know to be right, and humane, and true. Hence the work of educators is no less than the salvation of this world.

—Diana Chapman Walsh

College President
Massachusetts

It Is I Who Must Begin

It is I who must begin.
Once I begin, once I try—
here and now,
right where I am,
not excusing myself
by saying that things
would be easier elsewhere,
without grand speeches and
ostentatious gestures,
but all the more persistently
—to live in harmony
with the "voice of Being," as I
understand it within myself
—as soon as I begin that,
I suddenly discover,
to my surprise, that
I am neither the only one,
nor the first,
nor the most important one
to have set out
upon that road.

Whether all is really lost
or not depends entirely on
whether or not I am lost.

—Vaclav Havel

I spent most of the 1960s in Berkeley, watching history-in-the-making, working on a Ph.D. and preparing to be a professor. But I found the social movements of that era so morally compelling that, having finished my degree, I moved to Washington, D.C., and spent the next five years as a community organizer working for racial justice.

I never doubted the rightness of that work. But I grieved for the loss of my vocation as a teacher until I began to understand that organizing is simply teaching in another form: the classroom is the community, the subject is real life, and the students are all who are willing to be engaged—and some who get engaged willy-nilly!

I love "The low road" because it is a movement poem. It moves me through the gamut of feelings that come with passion for a good cause, not least the reform of public education. The first stanza is full of pain and fear. The second explodes into anger and the desire for revenge. The third brings things back down to human scale, and the saving grace of humor appears. And the fourth stanza gives me words to live by. Each day I ask myself:

- Do I still care enough to act, even when they say "No"?

- When I say "we," who do I mean?

- How can I reach out to someone else today—maybe even "the enemy"—so each day I can mean one more?

—*Parker J. Palmer*
Writer and Traveling Teacher
Wisconsin

The low road

What can they do
to you? Whatever they want.
They can set you up, they can
bust you, they can break
your fingers, they can
burn your brain with electricity,
blur you with drugs till you
can't walk, can't remember, they can
take your child, wall up
your lover. They can do anything
you can't stop them
from doing. How can you stop
them? Alone, you can fight,
you can refuse, you can
take what revenge you can
but they roll over you.

But two people fighting
back to back can cut through
a mob, a snake-dancing file
can break a cordon, an army
can meet an army.

Two people can keep each other
sane, can give support, conviction,
love, massage, hope, sex.

Three people are a delegation,
a committee, a wedge. With four
you can play bridge and start
an organization. With six
you can rent a whole house,
eat pie for dinner with no
seconds, and hold a fund raising party.
A dozen make a demonstration.
A hundred fill a hall.
A thousand have solidarity and your own
        newsletter;
ten thousand, power and your own paper;
a hundred thousand, your own media;
ten million, your own country.

It goes on one at a time,
it starts when you care
to act, it starts when you do
it again after they said no,
it starts when you say *We*
and know who you mean, and each
day you mean one more.

—*Marge Piercy*

Tending the Fire

THE UTILITY OF POETRY IN A TEACHER'S LIFE

Sam M. Intrator

I am a teacher in heart and in habit. And like most teachers I know, I move through the world foraging, borrowing, and accumulating that which will have utility in my classes and application to my students. I am shamelessly opportunistic—everything is potential fodder for my work. My file cabinets bulge with my harvests from the world: newspaper clippings, magazines, unit plans, journals. I even keep a blank videotape on top of the VCR so I can spring up from the couch and start recording some snippet that I can use in my classes.

So for the teacher in me, this work of collecting poems that teachers cherish and helping teachers share how they use poetry in their life and work represents a joy akin to what a naturalist must feel in a verdant forest or a furniture builder in the workshop of a fellow master. Woodrow Wilson once said, "I not only use all the brains I have, but all I can borrow." In this spirit, I have found myself eagerly borrowing many of the hundreds of ideas and suggestions that poured in by e-mail when we asked teachers to tell us how poetry matters in their lives and work. This chapter organizes some of the ideas, habits, and approaches to poetry suggested by teachers. It intends to be eminently practical, and I invite you to traipse through it as if you were strolling the beach. Pick up your colleagues' ideas, roll them through your fingers, pocket some, share some, or toss them away.

Poetry in Service of Turning Inward

Reading poetry, the teachers told us, helps host the conversations that matter most: our conversation with our dreams, values, and sense of being in the world. Poetry challenges us to examine whether we are living the life we most want to live.

Play with Poetry

Poetry often gets a bad rap as stodgy and highfalutin. Many teachers recommended this poem by Poet Laureate Billy Collins because it reminds them to lighten up, to not take poetry too seriously, and to let poetry speak to them in ways that are human and real.

I ask them to take a poem
and hold it up to the light
like a color slide

or press an ear against its hive.

I say drop a mouse into a poem
and watch him probe his way out,

or walk inside the poem's room
and feel the walls for a light switch.

I want them to water-ski
across the surface of a poem
waving at the author's name on the shore.

But all they want to do
is tie the poem to a chair with a rope
and torture a confession out of it.

They begin beating it with a hose
to find out what it really means.

Collins would approve of how the many hundreds of teachers who participated in this project describe their love affair with poetry. No torture or beating here.

Post Poems Where You Will Meet Them

Almost every teacher we heard from mentioned posting a poem someplace where they do their work. One teacher programmed the screen saver on her computer to display different poems. Karin Craven totes around C. P. Cavafy's "Ithaka" in her "take-me-along book"—a "constant companion whose contents of photos, poetry, and prose offer a sense of place and perspective along the journey." A college professor posted Walt Whitman's "No Labor-Savings Machine" on the back of his door so that when he leaves the office for the day, he remembers to ask himself "what gift he will leave behind for the world." The excerpt reminds him that while he may not be able to leave behind "any wealthy bequest to found a hospital or library," as a teacher he leaves "a few carols vibrating in the . . . air . . . For comrades and lovers."

Make Poems Part of Sustaining Rituals

High school English teacher and administrator Adam Bunting wrote: "Each year, sometime in August, I find myself with Adrienne Rich's poem 'Dialogue.' My ritual begins in the morning after the teacher-fever has crept into my dreams (you know the ones—teaching with no lesson plan, kids who don't respond to classroom management, finding myself naked in a school building). I awake consumed with anxiety and reach for the book and head outdoors. There I read, center, value, and turn inward. In doing so, I remember that I am a good teacher and can reach out to my students from a position of balance and strength."

A veteran high school teacher told of his annual poetry tradition: "Though I have been teaching for more than twenty years, my stomach still twists into knots before I meet my class for the first time. As I gather my books and papers, I recite these lines from Blake, which remind me that as a teacher I'm fighting a good fight and the weapons I brandish are books, chalk, and my open caring for my students. 'Bring me my Bow of burning gold! / Bring me my Arrows of desire! Bring me my Spear! O clouds, unfold! / Bring me my Chariot of fire!'"

Give Yourself a Daily Gift

One teacher joked, "A poem a day can keep burnout at bay." Many teachers described daily poetry habits connected to Web pages that send them poems each day by e-mail. These teachers set aside a time in the morning or the evening to be with poetry, a habit celebrated by Billy Collins in his project "Poetry 180," a collection of poems to be read each day by students for the 180 days of the school year. Our contributors suggested the following three Web sites as resources that provide a daily fix of poetry:

- Garrison Keillor's The Writer's Almanac,
  http://www.writersalmanac.org/.

- Poetry Daily, http://www.poems.com/.

- Poetry 180: A Poem a Day for American High Schools,
  http://www.loc.gov/ poetry/180.

Several teachers described how they keep thick poetry anthologies handy so they can leaf through the volume in search of poems that speak to them. Katharine Sims, a high school English teacher, described her encounters with sonnets: "I had an amazing Shakespeare professor in college who told us that he always kept a book of sonnets by his bedside because each was a perfect length and had a delightful thought to ponder just before falling asleep. This was a foreign idea to me, but because I so admired him, I bought a book of Shakespeare's sonnets and put them on my bedstand. I dusted the book for about two years. I opened and closed it now and then, beginning to question my sanity and that of my professor. One night, sleepless and stressed, I picked up the book and read the first sonnet to which the book had opened. You know the rest. Now I tell that story to my high school students, including the dusting and disregarding, and I give books of sonnets as graduation gifts, hoping that one sonnet will provide a revelation to one surprised human every now and then."

Turn to Poems in Times of Grief

Poetry can be a salve and guide in those raw and mournful times when a student dies, a colleague falls ill, or the world unravels. Teacher, principal, and now district office administrator Wendy Kohler told us how she seeks solace in times of sorrow and tragedy. "Be it the aftermath of 9/11 or the day after a car crash that killed two high school students—poems help. One poem I've gone to is Stephen Spender's 'The Truly Great.' Spender writes of 'those who were truly great . . . Endless and singing.' Be it a fallen leader, a favorite pop artist, a nameless firefighter, a young soldier from your hometown, or the student who sat in your English class—all can be named among the truly great. All were 'Born of the sun, they travelled a short while toward the sun / And left the vivid air signed with their honour.' All are worthy of memory and, when I sit with this poem, I can celebrate their greatness."

Vermont high school teacher Diane Bahrenburg told how Mary Oliver's poem "Wild Geese" has long consoled her. "On a cold November weekend a few weeks after my father died, I attended a teacher renewal retreat. Our facilitator passed copies of the poem around the circle. I glanced down at the first line: 'You do not have to be good.' I stared at the words and read them again.

I don't? I sighed. How simple. How reassuring. How profound. You see, I come from strong Minnesota Lutheran stock. My roots are anchored in generations of a Scandinavian work ethic that says I must always be 'good' and here Mary Oliver was telling me that I didn't *have* to be good. To a teacher prone to compassion fatigue from the pressure to be everything for every student, Oliver's words became balm for my tired spirit. I have learned it by heart. I have taped it to my desk at school and on my closet wall at home. I am grateful to have this poem in my life. It gives me courage."

Become a Poetry Collector

Teachers collect stanzas, lines, and pieces of poetry that speak to their hearts. These scraps become part of who we are. I keep a tattered laminated card in my wallet given to me by a high school junior almost fifteen years ago. It's a paraphrase from Goethe, and when those bleak moments come, and they always do, I read what my student wanted his teacher to know: "A teacher who can arouse a feeling for one single good action, for one single good poem, accomplishes more than he who fills our memory with rows on rows of natural objects, classified with name and form."

Another teacher, who works in a gritty urban district suffering from intense gang activity, shared how a Dylan Thomas stanza became her mantra. "I would find myself changing the line 'Do not go gentle into that good night' to 'Do not let them go gently into the good night.' It tells me to work harder and with more steel. It reminds me why I need to be a teacher." Another teacher taped the line "Life has loveliness to sell" from Sara Teasdale's poem "Barter" onto her steering wheel so that on the drive to school, she would remember that it was her job as a teacher to find what was beautiful in her children.

An elementary school teacher wrote that when she finds herself at the end of a long day and weary week, she turns to Mary Oliver's "The Summer Day." She told me, "I always linger on the line 'Tell me, what it is you plan to do with your one wild and precious life?' This line has special significance because I spend more time at school than I do with my family. When I read that line, I still answer that I choose to teach in my one wild and precious life, but to be honest, lately my voice quakes a little when I say it."

Think Like a Poet

Marie Frank, a third-grade teacher, infuses her classroom with beauty and kindles in her students a glorious love of language, words, and sounds. I know this because she was my son's third-grade teacher. Frank described how encounters with poems such as Lawrence Ferlinghetti's "Sandinista Avioncitos," which are constructed around metaphors, grab her and open up powerful streams of knowing about herself and her work: "The little airplanes of the heart / with their brave little propellers / What can they do / against the winds of darkness"?

Frank told us that her encounters with poetry provide her with a lens through which to view her teaching. "These lines are so emblematic of the resiliency of the human spirit. In my teaching, when students feel that something isn't going right for them, I gently try to give them the message that it is normal to feel challenged and to feel that some experiences are hard, but that they have the power to see themselves through these difficulties and that they will not stay at this place of questions and doubt. The 'winds of darkness' are a part of all of our lives, but the miracle is that we come out of these struggles ready to embrace life and fly with 'our brave little propellers' with all our hearts."

Revel in the Sounds of Poetry

The pace and beat of a poem is, according to Baron Wormser and David Cappella, what "gets a poem into us; it is visceral."[1] One teacher wrote, "I read my poems out loud to myself. Sometimes I shout them. Sometimes I whisper. But until I hear a poem I do not know it." Many teachers described how they attend poetry readings at libraries, local universities, bookstores, and coffee houses. Others shared several Web sites that provide opportunities for them to hear the soundwork of poetry:

- Robert Pinsky's Favorite Poem Project includes videos of poems being read, http://www.favoritepoem.org/thevideos/index.html.
- Poetry readings from Bill Moyer's Fooling with Words, http://www.pbs.org/ wnet/foolingwithwords/main_video.html.
- The Academy of American Poets has a listening booth where you can hear poets read their work, http://www.poets.org/booth/booth.cfm.
- Garrison Keillor reads a poem a day at the Writer's Almanac Web site, http:// www.writersalmanac.org.

Education professor Susan Etheredge told us that by reading poems out loud we can hear different voices in their own rhythm, cadence, and linguistic style. "In working with aspiring teachers, I want us to really hear the voice of the other. When we do this, it often challenges our notions of what is correct and beautiful. For this, I use a poem by Eloise Greenfield, an African American poet, titled "Honey, I Love."

> My cousin comes to visit and you know he's from the South
> 'Cause every word he says just kind of slides out of his mouth
> I like the way he whistles and I like the way he walks
> But honey, let me tell you that I LOVE the way he talks. . . .

Poetry in Service of Reaching Out

Poetry, teachers told us, also facilitates reaching out to others. The teachers who responded to our call for poems and stories described how poetry facilitates and provokes the essential conversations between teachers and those they work with and for in the school setting—students, colleagues, administrators, and parents. Reading and talking about poetry in community breaks down the isolation teachers experience when they close the classroom door and practice privately, shut off from colleagues and companionship. Poetry, for these teachers, is both an inspiration and an impetus to gather together. In doing so they discover how much they yearned for connections with their students and with the adults with whom they work.

Use Poetry with Each Other

Intermixing poetry into faculty meetings, school discussions, and other forums can enhance and expand the quality and depth of conversations. Judy Mayne Wallis, a language arts administrator from Houston, Texas, includes poetry at the bottom of every meeting agenda she creates. She said, "In my role as a language arts administrator, I often need to soften a message; enlarge a purpose for action; calm, comfort, or encourage colleagues; or use the aesthetic quality of poetry to help myself and others make sense of local or world events."

One teacher described how her school keeps a sign-up sheet for teachers to bring "the poem" for the faculty meeting. Another teacher described how her principal asks a different teacher each meeting to bring a poem that honors somebody else in the school community.

Linda Lantieri described a "found poem" activity to use with communities: "A poem is selected and each line is written on a small piece of paper. The group is convened in a circle and each person is given a piece of paper. The poem is read, one voice after the other. Encouraging individuals to really focus on delivering their individual line with zest and character can make this a potent way to bring a community together. In essence, the poem gives voice to the community. The poem can be read several times, which amplifies the impact of hearing the poem."

Marcy Jackson, codirector of the Center for Teacher Formation, often uses poetry in her work with teachers and reminded us to select poems carefully for use with groups. She encouraged us to ask the following questions in selecting poems: Is it relatively brief and to the point? Is it accessible? Does the poem contain aspects of both the personal and the universal? Is it one that will speak to others? Is there enough in the way of mystery, of rich content, or connection to questions of soul and role?

Other teachers spoke of the importance of providing ample time to process a poem. Writing or journaling about a poem prior to engaging in conversation helps generate ideas and disarm anxiety. An administrator who often uses poetry in meetings shared a series of questions that he uses to stimulate meaningful encounters with a poem: Where does this poem intersect with your life? What do you notice in this poem? What initially attracted you to this poem? What do you sense this poem is trying to tell you? What images, words, phrases seem to linger in your mind? Who would you give this poem to and why?

Give a Poem Away

Many teachers described how sharing poems—whether read out loud or distributed on paper—represents a special and generous form of giving. One said, "When I read and distribute a photocopied poem to my class or my colleagues, I give them a ticket to take a journey." Fred Taylor often gives David Whyte's "The Journey" and Naomi Shihab Nye's "Adios" as presents to his graduates.

Poems can also be gifts we give to those who are companions in our work. Jim Burke will occasionally send his friends poems via e-mail, tagged with notes such as, "No need to say more." Penny Gill copies poems onto cards and gives them as gifts and greetings to visitors. She calls them personal postcards. A second-grade teacher sends poetry postcards from the Poetry in Motion Web site, http://www.poetrysociety.org/motion.

Mary Cowhey, an elementary school teacher in Massachusetts, shared how poems can be a generous personal gift from one soul to another. Here, in a poem, she describes a series of poems she writes to a dear friend who is dying:

On Practical Uses of Poetry

The editors
would like some input
on practical uses of poetry.
Should I tell them
I write at least a poem a day
to a nearly dead friend and will
keep writing
keep mailing them
every day
even if
she can't read
can't write
can't answer.
Her sister will open them
and read them to her,
twice.
I will keep writing
because
my friend
loves a good poem
now and then.

"Yesterday morning, I mailed her another poem, like I have every day for the last three weeks, since she started taking morphine, which clouded her mind too much to read and write letters. I told her I could write her short poems instead, and she said she would like that. Later yesterday morning, she died. Saturday morning, I will read a poem at her funeral.

"Poems are a way to keep a promise. Poems are a way to send a secret message. Poems are a way to write a little and say a lot."

Poetry in Service of Social Change

Poetry may seem meek and inert in our efforts to forge better schools, but the teachers we heard from affirm that poetry can be a force in sustaining our courage to create more just and humane institutions. Poetry, as used by these teachers, helps give them a voice, a sense of meaning and collective courage, and readies them with both the verve and the desire to take on the institutional systems and bureaucracies that so often undermine our best intentions as teachers. Poetry, the teachers said, helps them join with others to work with devotion and heart toward making change and reforming the system.

Jump-Start Conversations That Matter

If enduring change is going to happen in our schools, teachers need time and opportunity to work and talk together. Brenda Abrams said that her department meetings had become yawning affairs marked by regurgitated "edujargon" that meant little. "We started launching our meetings with poems that had an edge, like Langston Hughes's 'Dream Deferred.' You should have heard the conversation change from hollow words about the instructional efficiency of homogeneity and tracking to what happens if we are complicit in drying up dreams."

Ken Bergstrom, a teacher educator from Vermont, challenges his pre-service teachers to think of teaching as more than mere craft and technique. Using Thomas Merton's "Cutting Up an Ox" helps Bergstrom challenge "the single-minded notion of many teacher preparation programs that teaching is mostly about applying techniques. It reminds me that the identity and integrity of teachers are paramount to good teaching."

Linda Toren, an elementary teacher from California, and her colleague Gary Thomas, a middle school teacher, have taken to e-mailing each other in "haiku and tanka as a way to keep each other inspired and hopeful—to celebrate and commiserate. Sometimes a longer conversation is too hard or we are too tired—a short poem can reach to the hardest places in an oddly effortless way." Here are some samples of their conversation about teaching and testing:

> when put to the test
> anyone might wonder *why*
> as if life might yield . . .
>
> —*Linda*

> passing the real test
> requires grace under bubbles,
> yielding to giggles . . .
>
> —*Gary*

> When the children laughed
> I smiled too, as they intend
> to blossom more than once.
> I plan to make it happen
> one way or the other.
>
> —*Linda*

Provoke Our Students

Sometimes a lesson is not so much about a fact, a skill, or an instructional objective as an effort to change the world and alter lives. As the grandson of Holocaust survivors, I felt a strange stew of potent energy, fear, and oppressive responsibility as I prepared to teach Elie Wiesel's *Night* for the first time. Perhaps sensing my panic, a wonderful teacher named Sue London came by my classroom days before I was to begin and did what colleagues do: she gave me her lesson plans and handouts. As I leafed through them, I came across a poem by Thomas E. Thornton that evoked my desperate sense of needing to teach this book in a way that would shake the cosmos and leave an enduring trace of its presence in my students' lives.

On Wiesel's Night

I cannot teach this book. Instead,
I drop copies on their desks,
like bombs on sleeping towns,
and let them read. So do I, again.
The stench rises from the page
and chokes my throat.
The ghosts of burning babies
haunt my eyes.
And that bouncing abaton,
that pointer of Death,
stabs me in the heart
as it sends his mother
to the blackening sky.
Nothing is destroyed
the laws of science say,
only changed.
The millions transformed into
precious smoke ride the wind
to fill our lungs and hearts
with their cries.

No, I cannot teach this book.
I simply want the words
to burn their comfortable souls
and leave them scarred for life.

Since the first time I taught *Night,* I have expanded my commitment to teaching teachers about the Holocaust and other episodes of inhumanity and humanity. When I work with teachers, I begin by reading this poem and telling my story. It is my way to share how sometimes we must teach things that burn in our belly.

Rob Kunzman uses Anne Sexton's "Transformation Poems" to help students understand how we are products of powerful social and cultural forces that shape our sense of who we are and in this case how we think of women. In Sexton's version of "Snow White," for instance, various images remind students that this is hardly the Disney version. The final lines drive Sexton's point home and create a new perspective for students about the way women are portrayed and shaped by societal messages. After the evil Queen has been vanquished, Sexton reveals Snow White's future:

Meanwhile Snow White held court,
rolling her china-blue doll eyes open and shut
and sometimes referring to her mirror
as women do.

Get Deep Fast

Meaningful and enduring change cannot happen without individuals' convening in community to speak to those potent hopes and concerns that live in the center of our hearts and minds. Teacher leaders use poetry to catalyze honest, edgy conversations.

Tom Vander Ark, during his tenure as a superintendent and now in his capacity as a foundation executive, has discovered that reading and sharing poetry allows him to get deep fast. He wrote, "Most staff meetings are superficial and administrative. To get to the heart of the matter, and do so within the constraints of school schedules, teacher leaders need strategies for going deep fast. Some people are skilled facilitators, some use books, some stories, some videos. For me, poetry is the most authentic (and effective) way to reach unexpressed memory—fear, doubt, anger, delight, awe, wonder—and make conversational the unmentionables."

Jay Casbon, president of the Cascades Campus of OSU in Bend, Oregon, used poetry in an interaction with a grant-giving foundation. Casbon's group had come up with some new ideas for addressing the literacy needs of a struggling neighborhood. The grant makers were typically cautious and suspicious of the unconventional approach. After some discussion, Casbon took out the poem "Magellan" by Mary Oliver and read, "For what is life but reaching for an answer? / And what is death but a refusal to grow?" "After I read them that verse, the conversation turned to 'How can we help?' I think the poem helped the foundation officials find the courage to fund our program."

As an organizational consultant, Linda Powell Pruitt uses poetry to enable others to step out of the box. "Teachers, principals, and board members come to me verbalizing a need to change but often they are very entrenched in a specific mind-set. They come in rushed and narrowly focused, and want tips and strategies. Asking them to work with a poem interrupts that mind-set and creates some space and openness. At the very least, it gives people a breather that can be filled with beauty and rhythm and hope. At its most powerful, the poem shifts their awareness to being able to 'study' that previous mind-set (its limitations, its dullness, its drivenness) and see how it blocks their creativity and ability to work together for change."

Forge a Common Mission

Poetry can give us common language and shared images that enable us to feel connected with each other and with the ideas at the center of our work and hearts. Joe Nathan, director of the Center for School for Change, uses poetry to create shared mission when he meets with educators and parents. "What these people often need is for someone or something to say, 'You're right! There's hope! The path you've taken may be less-taken, but it is very worth-while, both for you and for young people.'" He added that they begin each meeting by reading the following poem:

Think Different

Here's to the crazy ones.
    The misfits.
    The rebels.
    The troublemakers.

The round pegs in the square holes.
The ones who see things differently.
They're not fond of rules.
And they have no respect for the status quo.

You can praise them, disagree with them, quote them,
disbelieve them, glorify or vilify them.
About the only thing you can't do is ignore them.
Because they change things.

They invent. They imagine. They heal.
They explore. They create. They inspire.
They push the human race forward.
Maybe they have to be crazy.

How else can you stare at an empty canvas and see a work of art?
Or sit in silence and hear a song that's never been written?
Or gaze at a red planet and see a laboratory on wheels?
We make tools for these kinds of people.
While some see them as the crazy ones,
we see genius.

Because the people who are crazy enough to think
they can change the world, are the ones who do.

—*Courtesy of Apple Computer*

Preserve the Fire in Our Hearts

Our world needs teachers whose fire can resist those forces that would render us less just, less humane, and thus less alive. Poetry, by its capacity to touch the human soul and tap into the deepest wellsprings of our being, opens up opportunities for us to stay vital and alive. If we become too fearful to connect, if we become too isolated to reach out, if we become too preoccupied with the present to dream of tomorrow—we cannot teach or lead a movement well.

President of Wellesley College Diana Chapman Walsh wrote, "What I've come to believe . . . is that the leader's most crucial and most exhausting challenge is to maintain his or her own connections (to self and to others and to the purpose of the work), to resist relentless pressure from the system to be driven into isolation."[2] And so remains this inescapable truth: if we are to create vibrant and humane schools both for the adults who work in them and for the students who attend, we must begin by turning inward and then reach out to each other to forge the enduring and durable connections that make change possible.

While it may seem frivolous to enlist poetry as an ally on this path, the hundreds of teachers who participated in this project told us, time and again, that teaching was no mere job, but a labor of the soul honored and invigorated by poetry that helped them laugh, cry, dream, and teach with fire.

Endnotes

1. Baron Wormser and David Cappella, *Teaching the Art of Poetry: The Moves*. Mahwah, N.J.: Erlbaum, 2000.

2. Diana Chapman Walsh, "Toward a Leadership of Peace for the Twenty-First-Century Academy." In S. M. Intrator (ed.), *Stories of the Courage to Teach: Honoring the Teacher's Heart*. San Francisco: Jossey-Bass, 2002.

About the Courage to Teach Program

Under the guidance of Parker J. Palmer, the Fetzer Institute created Courage to Teach, a seasonal program of quarterly retreats for the personal and professional renewal of public school educators—individuals on whom our society depends for so much but for whom we provide so little encouragement and support. Courage to Teach retreats focus neither on "technique" nor on "school reform" but on renewing the inner lives of professionals in education.

Courage to Teach employs an approach to vocational renewal called *formation*. This approach is rooted in the belief that good teaching flows from the identity and integrity of the teacher. The formation process invites educators to reclaim their own wholeness and vocational clarity and makes connections between the renewal of a teacher's spirit and the revitalization of public education.

The Center for Courage & Renewal, an educational nonprofit organization, was established in 1997 to develop, deepen, and expand the work of teacher formation and Courage to Teach around the country. The primary mission of the center is to prepare facilitators to lead locally supported Courage to Teach programs. For more information, see our Web site at http://www.CourageRenewal.org.

All royalties from *Teaching with Fire* will be used to fund scholarships for educators to participate in Courage to Teach programs.

The Contributors

Maggie Anderson has been teaching biology, life sciences, and earth sciences to seventh through tenth graders for seven years and continues to be an advocate for children's voices in public education.

William Ayers began teaching in 1965 in a small free school associated with the Civil Rights movement. He is currently Distinguished Professor of Education and Senior University Scholar at the University of Illinois at Chicago.

Tracy Swinton Bailey taught high school English in Myrtle Beach, South Carolina, for six and a half years. On October 31, 2001, she gave birth to a son, Kyle, and has been working as a private consultant in order to spend more time with her child.

Jani Barker has taught children ages three through twelve for twenty-four years in rural and urban communities. Barker currently teaches first grade in West Linn–Wilsonville School District (Oregon).

Elizabeth V. V. Bedell is in her twelfth year of teaching in independent schools. Currently she teaches in ninth through twelfth grades and heads the English Department at Concord Academy, an academically rigorous half-boarding, half-day school in Massachusetts.

Curtis Borg has taught in the New York City schools for twelve years—six with severely emotionally disturbed children ages five through eight, and six with middle school children with learning difficulties.

Glynis Wilson Boultbee has been teaching since 1980—at a private school for children and adults with learning disabilities and at a community college (for seventeen years), and is now a traveling teacher and project coordinator taking arts and wellness initiatives into communities.

Adam D. Bunting, after teaching English for three years at Champlain Valley Union High (the school he attended as a teen), has enrolled in the Harvard Graduate School of Education. He anxiously awaits his return to the halls and classrooms of C.V.U. High.

Jim Burke teaches English at Burlingame High School in California. He has taught for fifteen years; authored numerous books, including *The English Teacher's Companion*; and founded and moderates CATENet, a resource for teachers.

Lucile Burt has taught at Arlington High School in Arlington, Massachusetts, since 1970. Currently she is teaching literature-based English classes to sophomores and creative writing classes to seniors.

Jay Casbon is CEO of OSU-Cascades, a branch of Oregon State University in Bend, Oregon. He is also a professor of education and vice provost at Oregon State University and a founding board member of the Center for Teacher Formation.

Mary Cowhey is a first-grade teacher at Jackson Street School in Northampton, Massachusetts. A former organizer, she is committed to multicultural and social justice education. She is a 2002 recipient of the Milken National Educator Award.

Sandra Dean has taught primary and pre-primary children for nearly thirty years, the last seventeen at Shepherd Elementary School in Hayward, California, a high-poverty area near San Francisco. Many of her students are immigrant children who speak English as a second language.

Debbie S. Dewitt has worked in the field of education for twenty-two years. Presently she is a kindergarten teacher at a public elementary school in South Carolina.

Lori Douglas has taught for seventeen years. She currently works with the Writers in the Schools Program at Ballard High School in Seattle. She still finds her small town roots and country kid chores to be a world away from her urban, street-smart students.

Caren Bassett Dybek has taught elementary gifted students, middle school remedial readers, and university graduate students for thirty years. She dedicates this piece to her fellow teachers at Comstock High School and to her Courage to Teach cohort.

Steve Elia has been teaching for fourteen years, eight in wilderness-based schools. Currently he coordinates Advancement Via Individual Determination (AVID) and teaches English at Bishop Union High School at the foot of the Sierra Nevada in California.

Susan Etheredge is an assistant professor of education and child study at Smith College in Northampton, Massachusetts. She is coauthor of *Introducing Students to Scientific Inquiry: How Do We Know What We Know?* (Allyn and Bacon, 2003).

Amy Eva-Wood has taught for ten years, as a high school English teacher, university instructor, ESL teacher, and teacher education instructor. Currently she is a doctoral candidate in educational psychology and coordinator of teaching assistants at the University of Washington.

Sarah Fay is an artist-in-residence at Teachers and Writers Collaborative, a nonprofit organization that sends writers into the New York City Public Schools. The children in her essay were from a subsection of the public school system reserved for children with severe emotional and physical disabilities.

Sandra Feldman, elected in May 1997, is the fifteenth president of the million-member American Federation of Teachers—the union's first female president since 1930. A former teacher, Feldman is widely recognized as an authority on urban education and an advocate for children.

John Fox has been teaching since 1984; he is associate professor at the California Institute for Integral Studies and adjunct professor in other graduate programs in the San Francisco Bay area, author of *Poetic Medicine: The Healing Art of Poem-Making* and is president of the National Association for Poetry Therapy.

Kelly Gallagher taught high school English for fifteen years. Currently he is English curriculum specialist for the Anaheim Union High School District and codirector of the South Basin Writing Project, and he teaches reading at California State University, Fullerton.

Catherine Gerber has been in the teaching profession for sixteen years. Currently she is a middle school teacher in a suburb of Seattle, Washington.

Penny Gill teaches European politics and political philosophy at Mount Holyoke College, South Hadley, Massachusetts. She has taught there for more than thirty years.

Theresa Gill taught for thirteen years at Mae Hensley Junior High in Ceres, California. She was the 2002 California League of Middle Schools Regional Educator of the Year and Stanislaus County Middle School Teacher of the Year.

John I. Goodlad is president of the Institute for Educational Inquiry in Seattle and professor emeritus at the University of Washington. He began teaching more than half a century ago in a one-room schoolhouse and has taught at every level from first grade through graduate school.

Stephen Gordon has been in urban education for thirty-five years. He is currently a literacy coach working with teachers and students at Snowden International High School in Boston, where he taught English starting in 1974.

Sam Grabelle works with The Big Picture Company and The Met high school in Providence, Rhode Island. For fifteen years she has worked and volunteered in education as everything from a preschool teacher to a grant writer to an after-school program director.

David Hagstrom has worked at almost every level in education for forty-five years: elementary school teacher, principal, associate superintendent, college dean, and graduate school professor. He is senior scholar at Lewis and Clark College in Portland, Oregon.

Sally Z. Hare has taught for thirty-two years in South Carolina public schools. She holds the Singleton Endowed Professorship in Teacher Education at Coastal Carolina University in Myrtle Beach, South Carolina, and is director of the Center for Education and Community.

Troyvoi Hicks has been in education for five years. He is founding principal of the Lionel Wilson College Preparatory Academy, which opened in 2002 as a secondary charter school within the family of Aspire Public Schools, California.

Marianne Houston has taught first grade through university in Missouri, Washington, and Michigan for forty years. She currently works with educators nationwide as a facilitator in the Courage to Teach movement in Michigan.

Janice E. Jackson has been in education for twenty-one years. Currently she is assistant professor in the Department of Teacher Education, Special Education and Curriculum and Instruction and in the Department of Educational Administration at Boston College.

Marcy Jackson codirects the Center for Courage & Renewal, leads Courage to Teach programs, and facilitates formation retreats. She has twenty-five years of experience as a child and family therapist, group facilitator, and teacher.

Rick Jackson codirects the Center for Courage & Renewal, leads Courage to Teach programs, and facilitates formation retreats. An executive with the YMCA for twenty-five years, he also consults on leadership development with foundations and nonprofits

Catherine Johnson is a full-time teacher of graduate studies at the Leadership Institute of Seattle. She also writes and works as a consultant, assisting individuals and organizations as they recreate their work in meaningful and productive ways.

Libby Falk Jones has worked in education since 1967. Currently she is professor of English and director of the Center for Learning, Teaching, Communication, and Research at Berea College, Kentucky, where she also teaches in the classroom, workshops, and community programs.

Edward Alan Katz has taught English in the New York City Public Schools for twenty-five years. He delights in teaching Shakespeare to his junior high school students.

Heather Kirkpatrick has worked in public education for fifteen years—first as a teacher in New York City high schools and then as a master's and doctoral student in education. She is now director of secondary education at Aspire Public Schools, California.

Susan Klonsky writes about education and the arts in Chicago. She is part of the Small Schools Workshop, an organization dedicated to creating smaller and more personalized public schools.

Wendy Kohler is executive director of secondary curriculum for the Amherst-Pelham Regional Schools in Amherst, Massachusetts. She returns to the classroom as often as possible and is currently teaching "Ethnic Diversity" to juniors and seniors.

Robert Kunzman spent seven years as a high school teacher, coach, and administrator in Los Angeles and Vermont. He is currently an assistant professor in the Indiana University School of Education, focusing on ethical education and teacher preparation.

Thomasina LaGuardia was a teacher of English and ESL in New York City public high schools for sixteen years and a teacher-consultant with the New York City Writing Project for fourteen years. She has been retired for the past year.

Lamson T. Lam is a fifth-year fourth-grade teacher at P.S. 198 in New York City. It is an urban school with an almost exclusively minority population.

Linda Lantieri has more than thirty years' experience in education. She founded and directs the Resolving Conflict Creatively Program of Educators for Social Responsibility and directs the New York Office of the Collaborative for Academic, Social, and Emotional Learning.

Laurel Leahy has been a teacher for around twenty-five years. For the past ten years she taught third grade in Dixon Elementary, a public school in Brookfield, Wisconsin. This past year she switched to kindergarten, her first love.

Katya Levitan-Reiner is a recent graduate of Smith College and former Teach for America Corps member. She is currently working as a substitute mathematics teacher, playing rugby, and exploring possibilities for the future.

Dennis Littky founded the Shoreham-Wading River Middle School in 1972 and was principal of Thayer Junior/Senior High School for thirteen years. In 1995, he co-founded The Big Picture Company to catalyze and support fundamental redesign of schooling and in 1996 co-founded and was principal at The Met high school in Providence.

Perie Longo has worked in education since 1962, teaching English, creative writing, and speech at all levels. She currently teaches grades K–12 in the California Poets-in-the-Schools program, and works in the private sector as a poetry teacher and psychotherapist.

Marian Mesrobian MacCurdy, writer, teacher, and singer, is associate professor and chair of the Department of Writing at Ithaca College. She has taught for more than eighteen years and is coeditor of *Writing and Healing: Toward an Informed Practice*.

Elizabeth Meador has been a teacher, tutor, principal, researcher, and professor since 1981. She is now professor of education at California State University, Monterey Bay, where she teaches the social, multilingual, and multicultural foundations of education.

Dan Mindich is one of the editors of the education journal *FacultyShack* and has taught English for fourteen years—first in rural Kenya, then in the San Francisco Bay Area and Vermont, and now at Punahou School in Honolulu, Hawaii.

Betsy Motten has been teaching for twenty-eight years. She is currently a fourth-grade teacher at Wallingford Elementary School in Wallingford, Pennsylvania.

Joe Nathan helped start the St. Paul Open School in 1971. For the last fourteen years he has directed the Center for School Change, which helps start innovative district and charter public schools and schools within schools.

Mark Nepo is a poet who has taught in the fields of poetry and spirituality for more than twenty-five years. He has written several books, including *The Book of Awakening*. Currently he is a program officer and poet-in-residence for the Fetzer Institute in Kalamazoo, Michigan.

Sonia Nieto is a professor of education at the University of Massachusetts, Amherst. For over thirty-five years, she has taught students at all levels. Her research focuses on multicultural education, the education of Latinos, and other culturally and linguistically diverse students.

Jeanine O'Connell has taught grades K–6 in Seattle Catholic and public schools. She is currently teaching a second-and-third-grade class at Highland Terrace School in Shoreline, Washington. She loves listening to children's ideas and reading their writing.

Parker J. Palmer is a writer and traveling teacher, author of *The Courage to Teach* and *Let Your Life Speak,* and founder of the Courage to Teach Program. In 1998, The Leadership Project named him one of thirty "most influential senior leaders in higher education," and one of ten key "agenda-setters" of the past decade.

Angela Peery has worked in education since 1986. She has been an assistant principal, a high school English teacher, an adjunct professor, and a district-level and building-level curriculum coach. Currently she is a teacher specialist for the South Carolina Department of Education.

Ron Petrich completed thirty years with the Minneapolis Public Schools, where he taught, wrote curriculum, and served as lead mentor teacher and as a professional development coordinator. He now teaches in the Education Department at Augsburg College, Minnesota.

Michael Poutiatine has been in education for nineteen years—seven in nontraditional, wilderness-based education and twelve in teaching and administration in independent schools. Currently, he is a doctoral student in educational leadership at Gonzaga University in Spokane, Washington.

Wanda S. Praisner has taught for twenty-nine years at the elementary school level as well as in continuing education courses and adult writing workshops. She is currently a poet in the New Jersey Writers Project for the State Council on the Art and Playwrights Theater.

Linda Powell Pruitt trained as a clinical psychologist and has worked for almost thirty years on organizational change efforts. Linda is currently on the faculty at the Leadership Institute of the University of San Diego's School of Education and works as an education and organizational consultant.

Rob Reich has worked as an educator for more than ten years. He was a sixth-grade teacher as part of the Teach For America program. He is currently an assistant professor of political science and education at Stanford University.

Leslie Rennie-Hill has more than twenty-five years of experience in the field of education. Currently she leads the high school initiatives at the Portland Schools Foundation in Oregon.

Libby Roberts is a thirty-seven-year veteran humanities teacher and adjunct professor of Composition and Literature at the University of Washington. She works as a high school teacher development coordinator for Everett School District's four high schools.

Samuel Scheer has been a high school English teacher for the past twenty years. With Rosetta Marantz Cohen, he has written two books on the history of the profession and how it might be reformed to attract and keep talented people: *The Work of Teachers in America: A Social History Through Stories* and *Teacher-Centered Schools: Re-Imagining Education Reform in the Twenty-First Century.*

Shifra Schonmann was a high school teacher for more than twenty-five years. She is now senior lecturer at University of Haifa, Israel, and head of the Laboratory for Research in Theatre/Drama Education. She has cowritten *Behind Closed Doors—Teachers and the Role of the Teachers' Lounge.*

Don Shalvey is a thirty-eight-year public school educator. He was superintendent of the San Carlos School District, where he created California's first charter school and co-founded Aspire Public Schools.

Ellen Shull taught for twenty-eight years in middle schools, high schools, and universities, and for fourteen years at the community college level. She is currently professor of English at Palo Alto College, San Antonio, Texas, and editor of the *Palo Alto Review*.

Theodore R. Sizer taught school in Boston and Australia, served as professor and dean at Harvard and Brown, and as principal at Phillips Academy. He headed the Coalition of Essential Schools for its first fifteen years and has published several books.

Judy R. Smith has worked for the School District of Philadelphia since September 1, 1979. She works as a special education teacher in an elementary school setting.

Sarah Smith has worked with young people in a variety of settings for the past fifteen years. She is currently the academic director of Rainer Scholars in Washington state, a rigorous academic enrichment program for talented students of color.

Ali Stewart is twenty-seven years old and has been teaching for three years and long involved in education through summer programs for disadvantaged youth, as a mentor and teacher for teenage Cambodian refugees, and as an athletic coach. She teaches middle and high school art and English at the International School in Dusseldorf, Germany.

Suzanne Strauss, a New Jersey native and Boston transplant, is now in her twelfth year of teaching high school. She lives and works in Northampton, Massachusetts, which allows her to commute by bicycle.

Lisa Drumheller Sudar has been a volunteer in all aspects of her children's lives for the past twenty-three years. She is a private music teacher and is currently enrolled in a Master in Teaching program through City University in Vancouver, Washington.

John J. Sweeney is in his sixth year as a first-grade teacher in the Wallingford-Swarthmore School District. He previously worked as a social worker in the field of mental health. He is a fellow of the Pennsylvania Writing Project, a writer, and a musician.

Fred Taylor has taught high school, college, and adult education for twenty-eight years. Currently he is on the faculty of Vermont College's M.A. program, and teaches in the environmental studies program at Antioch New England Graduate School.

Marj Vandenack taught for over twenty years in elementary schools in California, Illinois, and Nebraska. Retired from teaching, she is currently active in the Omaha chapter of the American Association of University Women, and she is the busy grandmother of three.

Tom Vander Ark is Executive Director, Education, of the Bill and Melinda Gates Foundation, He was one of the first private sector executives to serve as a public schools superintendent.

Tony Wagner, a self-described "recovering" high school teacher and K–8 principal, has more than thirty years of experience in education. He is currently codirector of the Change Leadership Group at the Harvard Graduate School of Education.

Diana Chapman Walsh is the twelfth president of Wellesley College, a position she assumed on October 1, 1993. During her tenure, the college has expanded its programs in global education, experiential and service learning, and technology-assisted teaching and learning.

Reg Weaver is a thirty-five-year classroom veteran. In 2002, he was elected president of the 2.7 million member National Education Association. He is an outspoken advocate for public education and one of the country's foremost African American labor leaders.

Tom Weiner has taught at the Smith College Campus School in Massachusetts for twenty-seven years, eighteen in sixth grade, as well as teaching high school at an Upward Bound program at the University of Connecticut in the summers.

Betsy Wice has taught in Philadelphia schools since 1964. For twenty years she has been the reading teacher at the Frederick Douglass Elementary School. For Wice, urban teaching is a useful way to share the pleasures of reading and writing with children.

Chip Wood has worked in schools for thirty-two years and is now principal of Sheffield Elementary School, Turners Falls, Massachusetts. He is co-creator of "The Responsive Classroom," a professional development approach, and author of numerous books.

Lesley Woodward has taught for about twenty years, mostly overseas, teaching English as a foreign language. Currently she is teaching ninth and tenth-grade college English at West Springfield High School in West Springfield, Massachusetts.

The Editors

Sam M. Intrator, assistant professor of education and child study at Smith College in Northampton, Massachusetts, is a former high school teacher and administrator and the son of two public school teachers. A recipient of the Distinguished Teacher Award from the White House Commission on Presidential Scholars, he is editor of *Stories of the Courage to Teach* and author of *Tuned In and Fired Up: How Teaching Can Inspire Real Learning in the Classroom.*

Megan Scribner is a freelance editor and researcher. She has developed, documented, and evaluated programs for nonprofits and has conducted research on what sustains and empowers teachers. She is the mother of two children and PTA president of their elementary school in Takoma Park, Maryland.